KUWAIT
in Pictures

Francesca Davis DiPiazza

Twenty-First Century Books

Contents

Website address: www.lernerbooks.com

Twenty-First Century Books
A division of Lerner Publishing Group
241 First Avenue North
Minneapolis, MN 55401 U.S.A.

web enhanced @ www.vgsbooks.com

CULTURAL LIFE 46

► Religion. Holidays. Social Networks. Art and Architecture. Music and Dance. Literature and Film. Sports and Recreation. Food.

THE ECONOMY 58

► Oil and Energy. Manufacturing and Trade. Services and Tourism. Agriculture and Fishing. Transportation and Communications. The Future.

FOR MORE INFORMATION

Library of Congress Cataloging-in-Publication Data

DiPiazza, Francesca, 1961–
    Kuwait in pictures / by Francesca Davis DiPiazza. — Rev. and expanded.
        p.   cm. — (Visual geography series)
    Includes bibliographical references and index.
        ISBN-13: 978-0-8225-6589-5 (lib. bdg. : alk. paper)
        ISBN-10: 0-8225-6589-7 (lib. bdg. : alk. paper)
        1. Kuwait—Pictorial works—Juvenile literature. I. Title.
    DS247.K82D57 2007
    953.67—dc22   2006018881

Manufactured in the United States of America
1 2 3 4 5 6 - BP - 12 11 10 09 08 07

INTRODUCTION

Less than one hundred years ago, only nomadic Bedouin people with their camels roamed the Middle Eastern desert land of Kuwait. Pearl divers and traders sailed the Persian Gulf waters off the small country's coast. The people of Kuwait were proud to be among the first in the world to embrace the religion of Islam. This faith arose in the A.D. 600s on the Arabian Peninsula where Kuwait lies. Here and there in Kuwait's desert, a dark, thick liquid seeped from underground and pooled on the sands. Bedouin herders used the substance to treat saddle sores on camels. But mostly it just got in the way when digging wells for a much more important liquid—water. In the 1930s, however, the needs of the world's industries and militaries demanded the sticky substance. Companies came to Kuwait looking for the dark liquid. Developers found that the nation sat on almost one-tenth of the world's supply of this valuable mineral—oil.

The petroleum (unrefined, or crude, oil) industry brought Kuwait great wealth, which rapidly changed the country. Within a generation, traditional ways of life were no longer necessary. Kuwait's forward-thinking

rulers, all from the Sabah family, poured the profits from oil into improvements for the country. They created employment, education, and health care for all Kuwaitis. Immigrants flooded into the country to meet the demand for workers.

In many areas, expanses of steel and stone replaced the sands of the desert. Trees that thrive in warm, dry places were planted along the city streets, and flower beds began to bloom. In the former fishing village of Kuwait City, the country's capital, the development since the mid-twentieth century has been extensive. Local industry, souks (outdoor markets), and shopping malls opened for business. Kuwait, with no rivers or lakes, researched and developed new technology to remove salt from seawater. Luxury cars and air-conditioned buildings replaced camels, sailing boats, and tents.

Although small in area, Kuwait is extremely significant in modern times. Most of the world's oil comes from the Gulf region. Kuwait's powerful neighbors, Saudi Arabia and Iraq, also have huge amounts of oil.

Kuwait has used its profits from oil to support regional security. But it has been unable to avoid conflict with its neighbors. During the 1980s, Iran attacked Kuwaiti oil and shipping operations because Kuwait supported Iraq in a war against Iran.

In 1990 Iraq's leader, Saddam Hussein, ordered his military to take over Kuwait in a dispute over oil, money, and land. This led to the first Persian Gulf war (1990–1991). During the war, an international force drove Iraq out of Kuwait. The invasion left Kuwait heavily damaged, but Kuwaitis rebuilt their country and economy. In 2003 the nation was the major launching point for a second Persian Gulf war—a U.S.-led invasion of Iraq to remove Saddam and his government. While this eliminated one of Kuwait's threats, the region has seen a rise in terrorism that threatens the peace of the Middle East and beyond.

In 2006 Sheikh Jaber al-Ahmad al-Sabah, Kuwait's ruler since 1977, died. The new ruler, Sheikh Sabah al-Ahmad al-Sabah, faces tensions between conservative and moderate groups in his country and in the Middle East. Conservatives resist the modernization that changed society so quickly. They believe that the Western influences that came with oil wealth erode the values of Islam. The most extreme people are willing to use violence to express their views. Moderates welcome many of the changes, including the 2005 law giving Kuwaiti women the right to vote. Kuwait's leader also seeks to keep the balance between Kuwaiti citizens, whose families have been in Kuwait since before the discovery of oil, and the non-Kuwaiti workers, who are not allowed citizenship. These various tensions will challenge the new government for the forseeable future.

THE ARABIAN PENINSULA

The Arabian Peninsula covers more than 1 million square miles (2.6 million sq. kilometers). This makes it one of the largest peninsulas in the world. It is 1,500 miles (2,414, km) long and 1,300 miles (2,092 km) wide at its greatest distances. The country of Saudi Arabia takes up almost 90 percent of the landmass. The climate of the entire peninsula is mostly dry, and Rub al-Khali, or the Empty Quarter, is the world's largest stretch of sand. The peninsula's Arabic name is *Jazirat al-Arab*, meaning "island of the Arabs." In the A.D. 600s, Arabia was the birthplace of Islam. Throughout history, however, world affairs generally did not affect the peninsula. Until the discovery of oil in the twentieth century, few outsiders were interested in the desert lands. Most of the peninsula's oil is found in its eastern portion, where Kuwait is situated.

THE LAND

The State of Kuwait lies in the desert on the northwestern coast of the Persian Gulf (known as the Arabian Gulf in nearby Arab countries). The country is one of five small but oil-rich Arab states that line the western Gulf coast. The other four are Bahrain, Oman, Qatar, and the United Arab Emirates (UAE). Kuwait shares no borders with these states. Iraq borders Kuwait to the north and west. Saudi Arabia forms Kuwait's southern and southwestern boundaries. Iran lies across the Persian Gulf from Kuwait but does not border it.

With an area of about 6,880 square miles (17,818 sq. km), Kuwait is slightly smaller than the state of New Jersey. From east to west, Kuwait's greatest distance is 95 miles (153 km). From north to south, the greatest distance is 90 miles (145 km). Kuwait's coastline is 120 miles (193 km) long. The Divided Zone (2,200 square miles, 5,700 sq. km) is a section of territory in the south along the Gulf. Saudi Arabia and Kuwait share this zone. Each country governs its own portion, but they share the zone's oil resources equally. Kuwait's territory includes nine small islands in the Persian Gulf. Faylakah is the only island in this group that people live on. Bubiyan is the largest island, but no one lives there because it is low-lying and marshy.

Topography

Kuwait's land is mainly flat desert with a few oases. Oases are places where underground water comes near the surface. The main topographic feature of Kuwait is the natural harbor of Kuwait Bay. The sheltered waters of the bay enable Kuwait City and other places along the shore to operate important ports in the busy Persian Gulf. Sand dunes, salt marshes, lagoons, and mud flats line the coast of the bay.

About 25 miles (40 km) south of the capital is the town of al-Ahmadi, located on a 400-foot-high (120-meter) ridge. This uplift

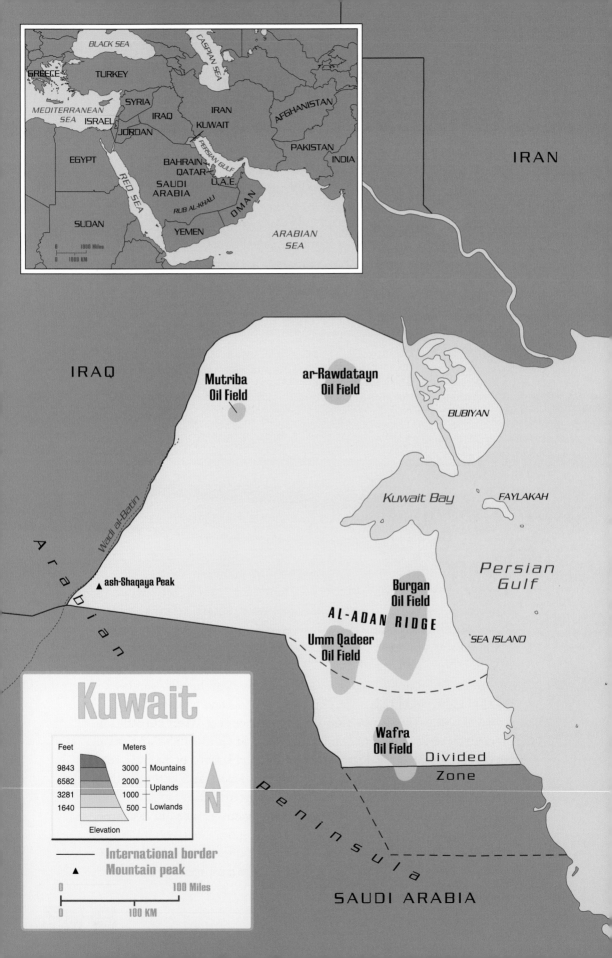

BLACK SEA

GREECE TURKEY

CASPIAN SEA

SYRIA

IRAN

MEDITERRANEAN SEA

ISRAEL

IRAQ

KUWAIT

AFGHANISTAN

JORDAN

PAKISTAN

EGYPT

BAHRAIN
QATAR

PERSIAN GULF

U.A.E.

INDIA

SAUDI ARABIA

RED SEA

RUB AL-KHALI

OMAN

SUDAN

YEMEN

ARABIAN SEA

0   1000 Miles
0   1000 KM

IRAN

IRAQ

Mutriba
Oil Field

ar-Rawdatayn
Oil Field

BUBIYAN

Kuwait Bay

FAYLAKAH

Wadi al-Batin

ash-Shaqaya Peak

Arabian

Persian
Gulf

Burgan
Oil Field

AL-ADAN RIDGE

'SEA ISLAND'

Umm Qadeer
Oil Field

Wafra
Oil Field

Divided

Zone

Kuwait

Feet	Meters	
9843	3000	Mountains
6582	2000	Uplands
3281	1000	
1640	500	Lowlands

Elevation

N

International border
▲ Mountain peak

0   100 Miles
0   100 KM

Peninsula

SAUDI ARABIA

and two others in the north interrupt the flatness of the desert. These high points allow crude oil to flow down from nearby oil fields to the coast. From there the oil is easy to export.

Lack of rain is evident everywhere in Kuwait. Only wind—which creates interesting rock formations—shapes and weathers the low-lying desert. A few salty lagoons line Kuwait Bay. In the southwest, the ash-Shaqaya Peak rises 951 feet (290 m) high. But otherwise, no major mountains and no rivers, lakes, or streams add variation to the desert landscape.

Climate

Kuwait lies in the same geographical zone as the Sahara, the world's largest desert. A high-pressure belt of hot air dominates Kuwait's climate. With a typical subtropical desert climate, Kuwait has long, extremely hot, rainless summers. Summer temperatures are regularly around 110°F (43°C) and may exceed 122°F (50°C). The temperature of the Gulf waters may climb over 100°F (38°C). In August and September, the humidity increases, making the heat more uncomfortable. Sandstorms and dust storms often occur between May and July but can come in winter too.

Winters are short, cooler, and dry. From November to April, the climate is mild, with a pleasant coolness in the evenings. In January, the coldest month, temperatures average between 50°F and 60°F (10°C to 15°C). In the interior of Kuwait, frost sometimes occurs. The temperature along the coast, moderated by the Gulf waters, remains warmer.

Most of Kuwait's rain falls in the winter between October and April. Although precipitation levels are unpredictable, the country only averages from 1 to 7 inches (2 to 18 centimeters) of rain each year. In a good year, enough rain falls to turn the desert green when seeds bloom in March and April. Some years see almost no rain at all.

Natural Resources and Environmental Concerns

Kuwait's most significant natural resource is petroleum. The country has an enormous petroleum reserve of about 96 billion barrels—almost 10 percent of the world's reserves. Only Saudi Arabia and Iraq have larger oil reserves. Natural gas found along with petroleum is a lesser but still significant resource. Kuwait also has plenty of sun and wind—alternative energy resources. Kuwait has developed some solar energy plants to harness the power of the sun, but the country relies almost entirely on its own petroleum.

Kuwait's location on the Persian Gulf is a valuable resource. Kuwait's natural harbor gives the country strategic importance to international trade and transportation on vital sea routes. Kuwait's coastal waters historically also provided pearls and continue to be a source of seafood.

Water is Kuwait's most pressing environmental concern. The nation's population has grown from about 200,000 people in 1957 to 2.6 million people in 2006. The need for drinkable water rose from 255 million gallons (965 million liters) in 1954 to more than 85 billion gallons (322 billion l) in the twenty-first century.

Several wadis, or dry streambeds that fill with rain during the winter, meet at ar-Rawdatayn. Rainwater collects in the wadis before evaporating or sinking into the dry soil. This water, along with brackish (salty) groundwater reserves, supplements Kuwait's water resources. Brackish water is used for industry, to irrigate crops, to clean streets, and to water herds of livestock. Distilled (purified) water is sometimes mixed with brackish water to decrease the salt.

With no permanent freshwater supply, the country relies mainly on huge desalination plants. Desalination is the process of removing salt from seawater. Kuwait is a leader in desalination technology. In distillation plants, seawater is heated. The steam rises, leaving the heavy salt behind. The steam is collected, cooled, and condensed in huge vats. This process is repeated over and over until the water is free of salt. Locally produced natural gas runs the plants. The plants' giant engines also produce electrical power for Kuwait's industries. The Doha Reverse Osmosis Plant uses reverse osmosis. In this system, saltwater passes through a special membrane under pressure, and freshwater is squeezed out of it. Desalination is very expensive, and in Kuwait water is worth more than oil.

Water pollution in the Persian Gulf is another environmental concern. Oil spills, pollution from industry, and the routine flushing of oil tankers threaten shore plants, birds, marine mammals, and fish. Industry and vehicles also cause air pollution.

Desertification (the change of already dry land into barren desert land) also threatens Kuwait's environment. A combination of human and climate factors causes desertification. Drought, clearing land of plant life, and overuse of dry lands contribute to creating desert. In Kuwait's case, damage from war is another factor in desertification.

Kuwait's environment suffered enormous and long-lasting damage from the first Persian Gulf war. The retreating Iraqi forces set fire to 749 of Kuwait's oil wells. Lakes of burning oil formed in the desert. It took international crews nine months to put out the fires. Heat, oil mist, and soot from the fires devastated all forms of wildlife. The black, toxic smoke spread air pollution as far away as India. Thousands of military vehicles during the war and firefighting equipment after the war tore up the desert surface.

Iraqi soldiers also released massive amounts of oil from oil terminals on the coast into the Gulf waters. The oil killed large numbers of the region's sea life, including birds, dolphins, and turtles. The oil slicks also destroyed miles of coastal and sea plants. The pollution reached beyond the waters of Kuwait to surrounding Gulf countries. It even affected Iran on the opposite side of the Gulf. International teams worked to clean up the oil and rescue animals.

During the Iraqi occupation, soldiers spread millions of explosive mines in the desert and the Gulf. In the following years, crews worked to find and remove the mines, but more still exist. Scientists estimate that the environment will take decades to recover fully from the devastation of war.

OIL FIRES

U.S. Air Force captain E. P. O'Connell described the oil well fires he saw two weeks after the end of the Iraqi invasion:

"On 13 March [1991], we drove through vast burning oil fields to another air base southwest of Kuwait City. It was a scene straight out of *Dante's Inferno* [a poem describing Hell]. Oil at times flowed like a river, 16 inches [41 cm] deep across the road. Fires blazed relentlessly on all sides. . . . The swirling black smoke from the fires on all sides of us was so thick we could barely see the vehicle 20 feet [6 m] ahead of us. I could feel the fire's heat on my helmet. Many of us thought our 'shortcut' could have been fatal. This was the worst of a 20-mile [32-km] abyss . . . . We were surprised when we came through the wall of black smoke into a clear sky."

—Edward P. O'Connell,
From the Line in the Sand, 156)

During the first Persian Gulf war, Iraq set fire to hundreds of Kuwait oil fields, severely damaging the environment.

Flora and Fauna

About four hundred kinds of plants grow in Kuwait. Though few plants can withstand the harsh desert, low shrubs and clumps of hardy grass survive year-round. After the winter rains, sheep and camels graze on plentiful blue and purple desert flowers that cover the wadis. When the land dries out, the seeds of these plants lie dormant until it rains again. The most common desert shrub is the *arfaj*, which may reach 3 feet (1 m) in height. A few remaining herders around Wadi al-Batin in the west use arfaj for firewood. Palm trees thrive near oases. Forests do not exist naturally in Kuwait, but trees have been planted in cities to provide relief from the scorching desert sun. Mangrove trees and sea grasses grow along Kuwait's coastal, marshy areas. These plants are able to tolerate salty water. They provide habitats for birds and other animals. The plant roots help stabilize the shoreline.

> Humans first grew date palms about 4000 B.C. on the Arabian Peninsula. The trees' fruit was a main source of food. Herders fed date pits to camels. They used palm wood and fronds (leaves) for building material, weaving, and fuel. Tough palm fiber provided rope. Many kinds of date palms exist. Some have old, colorful names, including Mother of Perfume, Bride's Finger, and Red Sugar. In modern times, palm trees provide welcome shade in cities.

Gazelles once roamed Kuwait, but overhunting has made them rare. A few kinds of smaller mammals survive in the desert landscape. Nocturnal animals are well adapted to Kuwait's climate. These creatures sleep in the heat of the day and are active at night. Several kinds of nocturnal rodents, including jerboas, gerbils, and hedgehogs live in Kuwait. They are food for wolflike jackals and fennecs, the world's smallest foxes. Rodents get all the water they need from the plants and insects they eat. Jackals and foxes get their liquids from the body fluids of their prey. Reptiles and invertebrates (animals without backbones) adapt to the desert too. Several kinds of lizards, snakes, and scorpions are desert dwellers. They burrow under the sand to avoid the sun. Birds and flying insects such as desert locusts travel long distances to find water. Birds of prey include short-toed eagles and kestrels.

In centuries past, the Bedouin raised Arabian horses. These horses have long been known for their beauty, grace, and stamina. Kuwaitis use modern methods to breed horses—including keeping DNA genetic records. They are proud of their horses' ancient desert heritage.

The adult fennec is about the size of a small cat— just 14 to 17 inches (36 to 44 cm) long. But its ears are much larger and suited to desert living. They help this tiny fox release body heat and hear distant prey.

Arabian camels, with one hump, were once a normal feature of desert life. Herders probably first domesticated wild camels about 200 B.C. in southern Arabia. Camels provided the main source of food (milk and meat), transportation, and fuel (dung). Since modern Kuwaitis live in cities, camels are no longer necessary. But Kuwaiti herders still raise them—along with goats and sheep—for meat and milk. Racing camels, like Arabian horses, are a living reminder of Kuwait's history.

Birds—including herons, swallows, skylarks, and wrens—breed or stop over along the Persian Gulf coast during their annual migrations. Socotra cormorants are shorebirds endemic, or unique, to the Gulf coast. Flamingos make their homes along the shore's mudflats. Some Kuwaitis keep falcons, which they train to hunt.

Persian Gulf waters off Kuwait teem with life. The Gulf near Kuwait is rarely deeper than 110 feet (33 m). This relatively shallow water promotes a diverse ecosystem (complex living environment). Sea grasses and algae are habitats for shrimp, lobsters, and many fish, including mackerel, snapper, grouper, and mullet. Shorebirds and migratory birds feed on the sea life. Fish caught in the Persian Gulf supplement the diets of both people and animals in Kuwait. Pearl-producing oysters also live at the bottom of the bay. Water pollution has endangered some fish and sea animals, including sea turtles and dugongs. Dugongs are marine animals related to the North American manatee. There are only a few thousand left in the Gulf waters.

Cities

When Iraq attacked Kuwait during the first Persian Gulf war, Iraqi soldiers damaged much of Kuwait City and other cities. After the war, Kuwaitis quickly rebuilt their cities and constructed new and more modern buildings. Kuwaitis have not forgotten the war, but few visible reminders of the invasion remain.

KUWAIT CITY Kuwait's capital, Kuwait City (also known as al-Kuwait), is a modern metropolis located on the country's main harbor. The oil-rich government built it as a showpiece of modern architecture. An estimated 413,170 people live there. Including all its suburbs, Kuwait City's population soars to 1.3 million. Hawalli is the largest suburb, with more than 80,000 people. It was built in the 1950s to house foreign workers.

Kuwait City thrives as an administrative, commercial, and financial center. Completed in 1993, Kuwait City's Liberation Tower is the city's tallest building at 1,220 feet (372 m). The tallest of the city's triple Kuwait City Water Towers rises to 614 feet (187 m). It holds about 1 million gallons (4 million l) of water. Modern hotels, shopping malls, and high-rise buildings stand alongside mosques (Islamic places of worship). The Grand Mosque, with room for five thousand people inside, is the largest of the city's hundreds of mosques. The area of the old walled city is the center of the modern business district. One block from the Grand Mosque, stockbrokers trade at Kuwait City's stock exchange building. The city's banking facilities are among the largest in the Middle East. Also in Kuwait City is the al-Qurain Martyrs' Museum. The exhibits are a tribute to one group of young Kuwaiti resistance fighters, nine of whom were tortured to death during the invasion.

The National Museum is another legacy of the destruction of war. During the first Persian Gulf war, Iraqis stripped much of the museum's important collection of Islamic art. Though Iraq eventually returned most of the collection, many pieces are damaged, and the museum building remains in disrepair.

Almost 100 percent of Kuwait's population lives in urban areas. Learn more about its cities, land, flora and fauna, and environmental challeges. Go to www.vgsbooks.com for links.

SECONDARY CITIES Al-Ahmadi lies about 25 miles (40 km) south of Kuwait City. An expressway connects the cities. Built in the 1950s to house oil industry workers, al-Ahmadi is near the important port Mina al-Ahmadi. (*Mina* means "port" or "harbor" in Arabic.) Home to about 27,000 people, the city is the center for the nation's oil production. Situated in the middle of Burgan Oil Field, the town sits on al-Adan ridge, which rises 400 feet (122 m) above sea level. Greenery, pleasant gardens, and villas set along tree-lined avenues grace the town.

Al-Jahrah (population 11,000) is one of Kuwait's oldest communities, built around an oasis. Evidence suggests that it flourished before Islamic armies conquered the area in the seventh century A.D. The Red Fort at al-Jahrah was central to the battle in 1920 when Kuwaitis defeated invading Saudi Arabian troops. Long an agricultural town, modern buildings have replaced most of the old farms.

Two modern towns, Sabiyah (or Subiya) in the north and al-Khiran in the south, were developed to house the country's rapidly expanding population after the oil boom. Sabiyah lies across Kuwait Bay from Kuwait City. Designed to house more than 250,000 people, Sabiyah includes schools, gardens, a hospital, and clinics. A road connects Sabiyah to other Kuwaiti cities. Al-Khiran is close to major centers of industry. Once an uninhabited desert south of Kuwait City, al-Khiran became a modern tourist resort with restaurants and playgrounds. Swimming pools, tennis courts, a sailing marina, and a ship repair yard are other attractions.

Faylakah Island (also spelled Failaka) lies 20 miles (32 km) east of the mainland opposite Kuwait Bay. Located at the mouth of one of the best harbors in the Gulf, it is 8 miles (13 km) long. In the 1960s, archaeological digs revealed traces of an ancient settlement on Faylakah. Scientists concluded that Greek ships had used the island as a stopover base. Extensive ruins of a city suggest that there was once an established population. What happened to these original inhabitants is a mystery. Before the first Persian Gulf war, tourists vacationed along Faylakah's sunny beaches, and many people lived and worked on the island. The Iraqi invasion drove residents from the island, however. Afterward, military bases closed the island to tourists, and only a few residents have returned.

HISTORY AND GOVERNMENT

Kuwait shares much of its history with other areas of the Arabian Peninsula. Its present-day boundaries were not fixed until the twentieth century. The growth of Islam—a religion established in the seventh century A.D.—was the dominant force in Arabian history. Historians know little about the region before the spread of Islam.

◉ Early Civilizations

Despite the lack of written records, archaeologists have discovered evidence of human existence in the area of Kuwait as far back as 5000 B.C. The people from this period were part of the al-Ubaid culture. They are related to the people who first settled and cultivated Mesopotamia (modern Iraq), between the Tigris and Euphrates rivers to the north.

From about 4000 to 1800 B.C., the Dilmun civilization extended along the coast of present-day Kuwait to the island of Bahrain in the south. The community made its living from seafaring raids and trading. At its peak in 2000 B.C., Dilmun controlled the route to India.

Traders carried goods between Mesopotamia and the Indus River valley in present-day Pakistan. The Mesopotamians regarded the city-state of Dilmun as a holy place whose people were blessed.

Dilmun's commercial power began to decline around 1800 B.C. At that time, invaders overtook the Indus River valley. They destroyed the culture there, thus ending trade with the region. Piracy flourished throughout the Persian Gulf during Dilmun's decline. Although Dilmun continued to trade, kingdoms in southern Arabia gained commercial control of the Gulf. After about 600 B.C., the Babylonians and later the Persians, based in present-day Iran, added Dilmun to their empire.

Greek Influence

After Alexander the Great of Greece conquered Mesopotamia in the 330s B.C., Greeks established a colony on the island of Faylakah. They named the island Ikaros after a Greek isle in the Aegean Sea. The site

ALEXANDER THE GREAT

Alexander (356–323 B.C.), king of the Macedonians, conquered the Persian Empire (present-day Iran). After an expedition to India, Alexander returned to Babylon (in Iraq). He intended to make it his capital. From there he turned his attention to Arabia and the Persian Gulf. He intended to create a navy that would dominate the Gulf and the Indian Ocean. When he died at the age of thirty-two, he was planning an expedition to conquer and colonize the Arabian coastline, including the territory of modern Kuwait.

probably began as a camp for Alexander's soldiers. Gradually, the colony became more diverse. Colonists settled on the shore. The Greeks built a temple to Artemis, goddess of the moon and the hunt. Because the island had military and strategic value, the colony expanded inland, where the Greeks constructed a fortress.

The Greek presence lasted for about two hundred years. Afterward, Greek control in the region declined. Eventually, the Romans entered the land around the Persian Gulf. After the Roman Empire accepted Christianity in A.D. 313, this new, monotheistic (one-god) religion influenced the inhabitants of the region. From this period until the rise of Islam, little is known about the area of present-day Kuwait.

The Muslim Conquest

In about 570, Muhammad—the founder of Islam—was born at Mecca, in present-day Saudi Arabia. Muhammad began preaching a monotheistic religion called Islam. Eventually, Islam gained many followers, called Muslims. They formed armies to extend the new faith throughout Arabia and to unify Arab peoples. By the mid-600s, the area of modern Kuwait was under Muslim rule.

During the early Islamic period, the main Kuwaiti settlement was on Kazima. This small peninsula in Kuwait Bay is near the present-day town of al-Jahrah. Because it was on the bay and had relatively fertile surroundings, Kazima

In the Zat al-Salassel, or Battle of the Chains, Arab armies led by Khalid ibn al-Walid defeated the Persians at Kazima in about A.D. 636. The event was so named because the Persian general bound his soldiers together in a chain to prevent anyone from fleeing during battle. The plan backfired, as the chain enabled the Arabs to kill every Persian soldier.

In the early Islamic period, **traders crossed the Arabian Peninsula on camels.** The traders carried goods from Africa and India.

became a famous trading station. Muslim travelers paused at the site to rest from their travels. Caravans stopped on their way to Mecca and other Arabian towns. During the seventh century, Muslim armies were stationed at Kazima because they valued it as a strategic point.

The majority of people on the Arabian Peninsula were camel-herding Bedouin. They were nomads, or people who move from place to place searching for water and grazing land. The Bedouin lived in a delicate balance with their harsh environment and did not develop urban settlements. They lived in tents the women wove from sheep, goat, or camel hair. The Bedouin had a rich tradition of passing on stories, poetry, and history orally from generation to generation. While centers of Islamic scholarship and book production arose outside the peninsula, the Bedouin of the desert did not write books. Therefore, many details about early Kuwait are unknown.

Lying at the center of a trade network, the Persian Gulf became an important commercial region. Maritime city-states developed and competed for control of the Gulf. A golden age of Gulf shipping began in the eighth century, when Muslim leaders (called caliphs) moved the political capital of Islam from Mecca to Baghdad, Iraq. Baghdad's location north of the Gulf made the waterway a favored trade route to the capital. Traders came from India and East Africa.

In the centuries after the rise of Islam, the harbor of Kuwait Bay continued to attract inhabitants to the region. With only dates, pearls, and camels making up the primary resources of the area, the people turned to seafaring activities to earn a living. They became expert sailors who knew the waters, the winds, and the location of dangerous reefs. Kuwaitis imported wood for boat making. They relied on fresh drinking water shipped or carried overland from other places.

In the sixteenth century, Portuguese, Dutch, and British seafaring powers entered the competition for control of the Gulf and its trade routes. These European nations were seeking wealth and new markets for their growing empires.

PEARL DIVING

Pearling was a major activity in the Gulf as early as the A.D. 800s. Kuwait's pearl trade reached its height in the 1800s. Traders sold millions of pearls yearly, mostly to Indian merchants. Pearl divers dove from boats to the bottom of the Gulf where pearl oysters live. They collected oysters in special nets hung around their necks. A nose clasp ensured they didn't breathe seawater. A worker called a *sayyib* stayed on the boat, holding a rope. When divers needed air, they tugged on the rope, and the sayyib hauled them up. Divers risked drowning, shark attacks, and damage to their ears from water pressure. In the evenings, the pearlers opened the oysters on the boat's deck. They sang songs while they removed and sorted pearls. Not all oysters produce pearls, and few pearls are big, lustrous, and round enough to be valuable. Divers had to stay at sea for months and haul tons of oysters to get a few pearls of great worth.

The Founding of Kuwait

Kuwait saw the arrival of a new group after severe drought struck the Arabian Peninsula in 1722. The lack of rain created a famine in the central Nejd region of present-day Saudi Arabia. Lack of food and water forced many Arab groups to migrate northeastward to the Persian Gulf in search of better pastures for their herds. The Bani Utub group was among these immigrants.

At Kuwait Bay, the Bani Utub settled at a small town they called Kuwait. The name is a form of the Arabic word *kut*, which means "a fortress near water." The area offered poor farming conditions and no nearby source of drinking water. But it had a milder climate and was less crowded than other regions of the Arabian Peninsula.

The Bani Utub mingled with the small population that was already in Kuwait. They participated in the trading activity on the Gulf. At least ten extended families made up the Bani Utub population. The Sabah family controlled the city of Kuwait. In 1756 Sabah bin Jaber was elected to be the first sheikh (leader) of the Bani Utub. (Descendants of the Sabah family have ruled Kuwait ever since.) When German explorer Carsten Niebuhr visited Arabia in the

1760s, he described Kuwait as having about ten thousand people and a fleet of eight hundred vessels. Most of the Kuwaitis made their living by trading, fishing, boat making, or harvesting pearls.

Development of Trade

The Kuwaiti-based Sabah family held a choice position for trade because land and sea routes connected Kuwait to commercial centers throughout the Middle East. Caravans from Aleppo, Syria, regularly stopped in Kuwait. This trade increased the wealth of the Sabah family and enabled them to build a strong fleet of ships. The Bani Utub also had strong trade relations with foreign powers, especially the British. Great Britain at this time was the most powerful colonial and trading power in the world. Therefore Kuwaiti merchants did not have to become pirates in order to survive. The location of Bani Utub merchants in a sparsely populated area gave them free access to both land and sea trade.

In 1762 Abdallah al-Sabah, son of Sabah bin Jaber, became Kuwait's second ruler. Abdallah, who ruled until his death in 1812, established patterns for future social and political development that lasted through the middle of the twentieth century.

Abdallah continued the friendly relationship with the British that his father had begun. In 1775 this friendship prompted the British East India Company to move its trading post from Persian-occupied Basra, Iraq, to Kuwait City. With the British trade presence in Kuwait established, British forces helped to defend the Kuwaitis against attacks from the Wahhabis of Saudi Arabia at the end of the eighteenth century. The Wahhabis were a group of desert fighters who wanted to purify Islamic nations. The British wanted to keep their influence in the Gulf.

Aided by the British, Kuwaiti merchant power became strong in the late eighteenth and early nineteenth centuries. Neither the Ottoman Turks, whose empire extended to present-day Kuwait, nor the Persians across the Gulf were able to challenge Kuwaiti control of the major trade routes. In the late nineteenth century, however, Kuwait's Sheikh Abdallah al-Sabah Jaber al-Sabah (ruled 1866–1892) recognized Turkish control of the region. He acknowledged the

Kuwait's first postal service began about 1775. The British East India Company began a camel service from the head of the Persian Gulf to Aleppo, Syria. Traveling overland across desert was faster than sailing around the Arabian Peninsula. This camel service operated until 1795.

Turks' power by paying Ottoman taxes and by accepting the title of *qaimaqam* (commandant) of the local Ottoman administration in Basra. Ottoman rulers in faraway Turkey, however, had little involvement in Kuwaiti affairs.

The British Protectorate

By the turn of the nineteenth century, Sheikh Mubarak al-Sabah (ruled 1896–1915) feared that the Turks might decide to occupy Kuwait. In 1899 he signed an agreement with the British accepting their protection and giving them control over Kuwait's foreign affairs. In exchange, Mubarak pledged that he and his successors would neither give up territory nor meet with officials from foreign countries without British consent. Thus began Kuwait's new status as a protectorate (a dependent state) of Great Britain. With British interests in the region formally secured, the British agreed to grant the Sabah family an annual payment.

Kuwait's northern border with Iraq dates from an agreement made between Kuwait and the Ottoman Empire in 1913. In 1914 Great Britain recognized Kuwaiti self-rule. The boundaries of Kuwait and Saudi Arabia began to take shape in the years following World War I (1914–1918). After attacks from the Wahhabis, who were trying once again to extend their realm, Kuwait reached a border agreement with Saudi Arabia in the Treaty of Uqair in 1922. At the same time, the two countries established a Neutral Zone (later known as the Divided Zone) along Kuwait's southern limit. They agreed to share the natural resources and the administration of this area equally.

The Discovery of Oil

While Kuwait and its neighbors were drawing their boundaries, British Petroleum, a British oil company, requested rights to test drill for petroleum in Kuwaiti territory. The early twentieth century's boom in industry and the use of automobiles led to a huge increase in the demand for petroleum products such as gasoline. Seepages in the desert indicated that oil lay beneath the surface. But only drilling could determine the quantity and quality of the deposits.

Gulf Oil Corporation of the United States was also interested in resources in the Gulf region. In 1932 Gulf Oil and British Petroleum formed a joint venture called the Kuwait Oil Company. In 1934 Sheikh Ahmad al-Jaber al-Ahmad al-Sabah granted Kuwait Oil permission to explore for oil.

Four years later, drillers discovered the second-largest and most productive oil field in the world—Burgan Oil Field—in southern Kuwait. (Only Saudi Arabia's Ghawar Field is bigger.) Exploration stopped dur-

In the late 1930s, oil tankers start coming to the Mina al-Ahmadi harbor.
These pipes fill the tankers with oil from Kuwait.

ing World War II (1939–1945). After the war, drillers found additional deposits at Wafra, Umm Qadeer, Mutriba, and ar-Rawdatayn, as well as at offshore sites. Kuwaitis, with the help of laborers from other countries, installed pipelines and other facilities. Commercial export of oil began in 1946. Control of these operations, however, remained in the hands of foreign companies, despite Kuwaiti leaders' efforts to take part in policy and management decisions.

Under the provisions of a 1951 agreement, the Kuwaiti ruler shared equally in the profits of the Kuwait Oil Company. This arrangement gave Sheikh Abdallah al-Salim al-Sabah (ruled 1950–1965) the money to start educational and public works programs for his country. Oil profits rapidly transformed Kuwait. The underdeveloped nation quickly became a superrich, well-equipped country with an extensive system of public services.

Independence and Conflict

Kuwait remained a British protectorate until June 19, 1961. On that date, Kuwait formally ended the agreement it had made with Britain in 1899, thereby achieving full independence. Sheikh Abdallah added the title of emir (ruler) to his name. The new State of Kuwait joined the Arab League. The leaders of Arab states had formed the league to strengthen Arab ties and to address Arab concerns. On November 11, 1962, Emir Sheikh Abdallah approved a Kuwaiti constitution written by a constitutional assembly.

During the 1960s, Kuwait became increasingly wealthy as the nation's output of petroleum rose. Government policies sought to fairly distribute income and land among Kuwaiti citizens through generous welfare programs. Along with steady domestic improvements, however, the country faced regional conflicts.

For many years, Kuwait was an active supporter of the Arab cause against Israel, a nation on the Mediterranean Sea. Israel was formed in 1948 to create a homeland for the Jewish people. Kuwait, like the rest of the Arab world, believed that the creation of Israel was an injustice against Palestinian Arabs who lived on the land. Many Palestinians emigrated from Israel to other countries, including Kuwait.

In 1973 an Arab-Israeli war broke out. Kuwait and other Arab oil-producing countries cut back shipments of oil to countries that supported Israel. Called an embargo, the halt of oil shipments affected consumers throughout the United States and Europe. The Organization of Petroleum Exporting Countries (OPEC) also imposed a 70 percent increase in oil prices. Kuwait is a member of OPEC.

Emir Sheikh Jaber al-Ahmad al-Sabah was born in 1926. He ruled Kuwait from 1977 until his death in 2006.

In 1979 the Islamic Revolution in Iran declared that country to be an Islamic republic. The new Iranian government made Islam the law of the land. That same year, secular (nonreligious) leader Saddam Hussein became president of Iraq. A war between Iran and Iraq erupted in 1980 over territory and other issues. The nearby war threatened the production and transport of Kuwait's oil. It also complicated the country's foreign policies in the region. Although Kuwait declared neutrality in this war, it supplied Iraq with billions of dollars of loans and aid. Kuwait also allowed foreign vessels carrying arms for Iraq to unload in Kuwait City. Kuwait wanted to stay on good terms with its powerful neighbor Iraq. The people also share religious and cultural ties that they do not share with Iranians.

This support of Iraq made Iran hostile toward Kuwait. Pro-Iranian groups led terrorist attacks on Kuwaitis. In 1985 an Islamic militant (a violent supporter of Islam as a political force) drove a car bomb into a parade in a failed attempt to assassinate Emir Sheikh Jaber al-Ahmad al-Sabah. Iran also bombed Kuwait's oil installations and shipping operations in the Persian Gulf. In 1987 Kuwait called on the United States to escort oil tankers and other ships through the Persian Gulf. This protection enabled Kuwait to continue its vital international trade. The Iran-Iraq War ended in 1988. Both countries suffered enormous loss of life and economic damage.

The First Persian Gulf War

Although Kuwait had supported Iraq during the Iran-Iraq War, tensions increased between Kuwait and Iraq in the late 1980s. During the 1960s and 1970s, Iraq had questioned the old Ottoman boundary and made claims to Kuwaiti territory. Iraq began to make these claims again. Another cause of tension was the decline of Iraq's oil revenues. Iraq insisted that the decline was the result of Kuwait producing more oil than OPEC quotas allowed and therefore driving down world oil prices. Iraq also accused Kuwait of stealing oil from an oil field that straddles the Iraq-Kuwait border. Kuwait admitted that it was removing the oil. But Kuwaiti leaders said the country was doing so because Iraq was not repaying its loans to Kuwait. Iraq insisted Kuwait should forgive the loans. At a meeting on August 1, 1990, the two countries failed to resolve their disputes. On August 2, under Saddam's orders, about 100,000 Iraqi troops invaded Kuwait.

Kuwait's military was unprepared, and Iraq quickly seized Kuwait's oil wells and shipping facilities. Iraqi soldiers looted Kuwaiti homes, museums, hospitals, and public buildings. They sent valuable items back to Iraq. Many buildings and public works were bombed or burned. Almost half the population of Kuwait took refuge in other countries.

Most of the ruling family fled to Saudi Arabia, where they established a government in exile. Fahd al-Ahmad, one of the emir's brothers, lost his life leading troops against the Iraqi invaders. People who remained in Kuwait faced food and water shortages and the harsh treatment of Iraqi occupiers. The Iraqi soldiers arrested, tortured, and killed people they suspected of being part of a resistance movement. Iraq also moved troops to the Saudi Arabian border. Many world leaders feared an invasion of Saudi Arabia.

The United Nations (UN) was quick to condemn the attack and authorize a military response. Thirty-nine countries, including Egypt, Syria, and other Arab nations, massed troops in Saudi Arabia to protect the region. Led by the United States, this defense was called Operation Desert Shield. The UN imposed a deadline of January 15, 1991, for Iraq to withdraw from Kuwait. When Iraq did not withdraw, the allied forces launched an attack against Iraq called Operation Desert Storm. Using advanced weapons systems, the allies easily defeated Iraqi forces in a forty-two-day air war followed by a one-hundred-hour ground war. On February 26, Kuwaiti and allied soldiers entered Kuwait City, ending the conflict.

The United Nations made the Kuwait-Iraq border official in 1991 after the war. Kuwait began repairing war damage immediately. Retreating

U.S. Marines arrive on the Arabian Peninsula for **Operation Desert Shield** in 1990.

Iraqi soldiers had set fire to hundreds of oil wells. They had also released more than 160 million gallons (606 million l) of oil into the Persian Gulf. Specially trained crews managed to put out the disastrous fires within nine months. Crews from around the world cleaned up the oil spill over a longer period of time. To pay for the reconstruction costs of $20 billion, Kuwait cashed in many of its foreign investments and borrowed money from other countries. Damaged wells prevented the country from producing oil—its main source of income—for several months.

Postwar Events

Following the first Persian Gulf war, some Kuwaitis pushed for immediate political reform. They wanted more open, Western-style democracy, including free speech. Emir Sheik Jaber, however, put off elections for the legislature, called the National Assembly. He maintained that rebuilding the country was more important.

At the same time, strong resentment existed toward Kuwait's large Palestinian community. Leaders of the Palestinian Liberation Organization (PLO) had supported Saddam Hussein's actions. Therefore, Kuwaitis suspected Palestinians of working with Iraqis during the war, though some had also aided Kuwaitis. Kuwaiti police and military officers killed hundreds of Palestinians—and other people whom they suspected of sympathizing with Iraq—without trial.

Along with the PLO, leaders of several Arab countries—including Sudan, Jordan, and Yemen—had not opposed Saddam's invasion of Kuwait. After the war, Kuwait's relations with these countries were slow to recover. Workers from these countries were forbidden entry into Kuwait. Thousands of Palestinians and other Arabs were not allowed to return to the country. In many cases, Palestinian families had lived in

OIL DUMPING STOPPED

During the first Persian Gulf war, a Kuwait Oil Company superintendent named Khalid al-Othman worked at the Mina al-Ahmadi oil refinery. Three days after the coalition started bombing, Iraqi occupiers began to release Kuwait's stored oil into the Persian Gulf. Millions of barrels eventually flooded the waters. Al-Othman told *National Geographic* magazine how he and three other Kuwaitis risked their lives to keep even more oil from polluting the Gulf. A 12-foot (4-m) pipe carried oil from the Mina al-Ahmadi storage tanks to Sea Island. One night, al-Othman and his helpers, working secretly to avoid spies, closed a valve that the Iraqis didn't know about and changed the sign on the valve to read "open." When the Iraqis released the main spill of oil by dynamiting Sea Island, the closed valve held back 8.5 million barrels of oil.

Kuwait since 1948, when the creation of Israel replaced Palestine. The government's policy left many industries with labor shortages. To solve this problem, the country gradually ended its restrictions on immigration. However, officials sought workers from outside the Arab world. Indian, Pakistani, Korean, Thai, and Filipino workers came in large numbers.

In October 1992, democracy advanced when Kuwaitis elected a new National Assembly. Many of its members opposed the Sabah government and challenged its laws. Although the elected assembly increased its voice in governing Kuwait, the emir could disband it at any time. Along with the return of political vitality, repair of most of Kuwait's transportation and communications systems, businesses, public buildings, and residential areas was complete by the end of 1993.

Kuwait's relations with Iraq remained tense. Kuwait charged that Iraq held 625 Kuwaiti prisoners of war. Many Kuwaitis feared that Saddam Hussein would attempt to take Kuwait again. To discourage an attack, Kuwait built a trench protected by land mines and electronic monitors along the Kuwait-Iraq boundary. UN forces patrolled this border. For additional protection, Kuwait signed defense agreements with the United States, Great Britain, and France. The country also modernized its own

Iraqi soldiers burned buildings as they left Kuwait City. This scorched building was the office of the emir of Kuwait.

military. Iraq officially recognized the Kuwait-Iraq boundary in 1994. But Iraq's leadership continued to condemn Kuwait for its friendly relations with the United States.

During the 1990s, Kuwait modernized in many ways. The nation replaced old technology and infrastructure that had been damaged by the war with new and better equipment and public works. Many Kuwaitis also pushed to build a more democratic government, including equal rights for women. Efforts to gain the vote for women, however, faced strong opposition from conservative religious groups. These groups disapproved of the modernization of Kuwaiti society. In 1999 the emir, Sheikh Jaber, issued a decree giving women the right to vote. The National Assembly defeated the decree by a small number of votes.

The Second Persian Gulf War

In the years after the first Persian Gulf war, Saddam Hussein did not fulfill the cease-fire agreements he had signed with the UN. He did not cooperate with UN weapons inspectors searching for weapons of mass destruction in Iraq. The United States became especially concerned about illegal weapons after terrorists attacked the United States on September 11, 2001. U.S. president George W. Bush worried that Saddam might supply terrorists with weapons. Kuwait strongly condemned the September 11 attacks.

Despite disagreements among UN member countries, in early 2003, a U.S.-led coalition prepared to invade Iraq to remove Saddam Hussein. Kuwait served as a major partner. The nation allowed coalition forces to use 60 percent of its land and provided troops and fuel assistance.

On March 20, 2003, the second Persian Gulf war (also called Operation Iraqi Freedom) began, with intensive bombing of Iraq. On April 9, coalition forces took charge of Baghdad, Iraq's capital, and Saddam's government fell. Kuwait pledged $1.5 billion toward reconstruction in Iraq and remained an important transit route in and out of Iraq.

In the years after the removal of Saddam, Kuwait stays watchful because Iraq remains very unstable. No weapons of mass destruction were found, but terrorism in the Gulf region increased. Kuwait's government is an important partner with the United States in the global efforts against terrorism. Kuwait's security forces have clashed with well-armed militants. Some militants in Kuwait have links to al-Qaeda, the terrorist network mainly responsible for the September 11, 2001, attacks on the United States. Among other issues, the militants disapprove of the United States' support of Israel. They want the military forces and the businesses of Western nations, especially the United States, to leave the Middle East. They also want to establish conservative Islamic governments in Arab nations such as Kuwait.

New Voters and a New Emir

In a move to strengthen democracy, in May 2005, Kuwait's lawmakers voted to grant women Kuwaiti citizens the right to vote and to run for political office. The majority of Kuwaitis still cannot vote, however, because they are not allowed to be citizens.

One month after the historic decision, Prime Minister Sheikh Sabah appointed Massouma al-Mubarak to be the first woman member of the cabinet (group of government advisers). Conservative members strongly opposed the appointment, shouting in protest when al-Mubarak was sworn-in.

Kuwaitis mourned when Sheikh Jaber died on January 15, 2006. Viewed as a skilled politician, he had become Kuwait's thirteenth ruler from the Sabah family in 1977. With the ruling family's support, Kuwait's cabinet nominated Prime Minister Sheikh Sabah al-Ahmad al-Sabah as emir. Sabah had been running day-to-day affairs while Jaber was ill.

Kuwait's traditional society has undergone changes at a fast pace since the discovery of oil. Wars in the region have also changed traditional alliances, including forming strong ties between Kuwait and the United

When **Emir Sheikh Jaber al-Ahmad al-Sabah died in 2006,** Kuwait declared forty days of mourning. Mourners carried his image through the streets of Kuwait City.

States. The new emir faces high tensions at home and abroad between moderates, who support modern changes, and conservatives, who want to keep the old ways.

Read more about the conflicting forces that have shaped Kuwait's history and government from its beginnings in 5000 B.C. Visit www.vgsbooks.com for links.

Government

Kuwait is an independent state that operates under a hereditary monarchy—that is, the emir is chosen by and from the ruling family. The emir appoints a relative to serve as prime minister and another to succeed the monarch to the throne. The constitution guarantees equal opportunities, individual freedom, and freedoms of religion and the press "within the limits of the law." For example, it is illegal to insult Allah (Arabic for "God") or the prophet Muhammad. It also protects the freedom to form societies and trade unions. Government powers are separated into three branches—executive, legislative, and judicial.

The emir governs through a cabinet of ministers. His appointed prime minister leads and chooses the cabinet ministers. The prime minister and other cabinet members are responsible to the emir for matters concerning general policy.

In 1992 the emir allowed the election of a legislative body, the fifty-member National Assembly. Members serve four-year terms. An elected assembly had served twice before—from 1963 to 1976 and from 1981 to 1986. Both times, however, the emir dissolved it when representatives voiced too much opposition to his policies. Only literate Kuwaiti citizens are allowed to vote. Women citizens voted for the first time in the 2006 parliamentary elections.

In 1959 Kuwaiti officials reorganized the judicial system—which is based on Islamic law, or Sharia—by establishing courts of law and by adopting modern legal codes. Two kinds of courts exist in Kuwait. Courts of first instance decide personal, civil, commercial, and criminal cases. Courts of appeal rehear cases from the lower courts. Appeals from this secondary level go to the Supreme Court, which also rules on the constitutionality of laws. The emir acts as the final source of judicial appeal, and he has the power to pardon those who have been convicted.

THE PEOPLE

Kuwait's Citizenship Law allows only about half of the 2.6 million people living in Kuwait to become full Kuwaiti citizens. Citizens are people whose families lived in Kuwait before 1920. The remaining 1.3 million people are from other countries or descended from families who moved to Kuwait for work. The government wants to protect Kuwait's traditional society and to keep political power in the hands of the original Kuwaiti families and clans. They fear being controlled or changed by the numerous noncitizens. Nevertheless, in 1996 the government extended the right to vote. It gave the vote to the small number of men who do not meet the pre-1920 requirement but have lived and worked in Kuwait for thirty years. Kuwait's economy depends on noncitizens. They supplement the nation's workforce with their expertise in science, medicine, engineering, and other fields. They also do most of the poorly paid work.

The population continues to grow with new immigrants and new births. A woman in Kuwait will give birth to an average of four children

in her lifetime. Experts estimate that Kuwait's population will reach more than 7 million by the year 2050.

Social Structure

Kuwait traditionally has ordered its society according to clan, or tribal, loyalties. Clans are large family groups sharing a common ancestor. Traditionally, a person's place in the clan was more important than job or riches. However, social change has made its mark on the country. Widespread economic growth has made traditional social relationships less important. Money can buy necessities and conveniences that in the past could only be had through family connections. War has also rearranged social structures and family loyalties. Furthermore, the growth of the capital city has reinforced the nation's urban character. Few Kuwaitis still lead the nomadic lifestyle of their Arab ancestors. In fact, essentially 100 percent of the population live in cities. Kuwait's population density is 339 people per square mile (131 per sq. km).

ARABS

What does it mean to be an Arab? Definitions vary, but most people agree that an Arab is a person whose first language is Arabic and who feels a part of Arab history and culture. They may live anywhere in the world. Arabs in the Arabian Peninsula, including Kuwait, feel special pride because they are the descendants of the original Arabs, who were camel-herding nomads on the peninsula. These people called themselves *Bedu*. The French turned "Bedu" into the name "Bedouin." (*Bedu* can also mean "desert" in Arabic.) With the spread of Islam, people in other parts of the Middle East and the world adopted the Arabic language and culture. Arabs do not all belong to the religion of Islam, and not all Muslims are Arabs. (In fact, the country with the largest Muslim population is Indonesia in Southeast Asia.) But most Arabs at least hold the religion in special regard, since it originated on the Arabian Peninsula.

Kuwaiti citizens, many of Bedouin ancestry, are a privileged and well-off class. They benefit from one of the best-developed welfare states in the world. Status among Kuwaitis is determined by religious affiliation, by ethnic background, and by the date they or their ancestors immigrated to Kuwait.

Nevertheless, a class structure has taken shape alongside the age-old family system of social organization. Kuwaitis are taking advantage of the opportunities of free education. Good education places professional jobs within the reach of all citizens, thereby increasing social mobility. Many ambitious Kuwaitis from modest backgrounds have achieved great prosperity. Although family connections have long played an important role in an individual's opportunities, personal ability increasingly shapes a person's future.

Kuwaiti citizens have reserved many of the best jobs for themselves, leaving unskilled positions for noncitizens. Some noncitizens fill skilled positions when no Kuwaitis have the proper training. But the differences between these two groups are very clearly maintained. Noncitizens generally live in separate areas and mostly have no political or voting rights.

Noncitizens are also restricted in the ownership of businesses and property and receive lower wages than Kuwaitis for equivalent work. Along with Kuwaiti citizens, noncitizens receive free education and health care, but they are excluded from other welfare programs, such as housing allowances and pensions (retirement savings plans).

Immigrant laborers unload fish from a boat in Kuwait Bay.

Most of the people who once held industrial jobs were noncitizens, and many were not allowed to return to Kuwait after the first Persian Gulf war. Many of the Palestinians—who made up 20 percent of the prewar population—held high positions in the government and other fields. During the war, some Palestinians sympathized with Iraq. As a result, widespread distrust of Palestinians exists among Kuwaiti citizens. To restrain the power of noncitizens, the government has increased its ratio of non-Arab workers in Kuwait by recruiting workers from Asia. Non-Arabs include people from India, Pakistan, the Philippines, Sri Lanka, South Korea, and Thailand. People from Iran, who also are not Arabs, make up about 4 percent of Kuwait's population.

Since the mid-twentieth century, Kuwait's social structure has been divided into citizens and noncitizens called *bidounis*. This word is short for *bidoun jinsiyya* meaning "without nationality."

Many noncitizens would rather live in Kuwait than in their less developed native countries because they can earn more money in the oil-rich nation. Indeed, Kuwait's average per capita (per person) income of $19,510 is about the average for European countries. But many noncitizens work in low-paid jobs, such as manual labor, restaurant work, taxi driving, and servant jobs.

CLOTHING

Clothing in Kuwait evolved to protect people from the harsh desert climate and also to meet Islamic codes of modesty. Many Kuwaitis dress in traditional styles. A man usually wears a loose-fitting robe called a *dishdasha*, with long sleeves and buttons up to the throat. He may wear a wool or camel-hair cloak called a *bisht* in cool weather. A square cloth worn on a man's head is called a *ghutra*. A dark cord called an *iqal* holds the cloth in place.

At home, women often wear Western-style clothing, such as jeans or dresses. Out in public, a woman may choose to cover herself in various ways. She may cover her head with a head scarf called a *hijab*. She may veil her face. Or she may cover herself from head to toe in a robe called an *abaya*. Covering remains common—even required—in other Gulf Arab states. But more and more Kuwaiti women are choosing not to cover themselves.

◉ Family Life and Women

Arab society is patriarchal. That is, men are in charge. The unifying factor in Kuwaiti society is the family, with the father at its head. Kuwaitis hold family in higher esteem than they do the individual, the community, or the state. As in other Arab cultures, the traditional family unit is extended. Islam allows a man to have up to four wives, if he can support them all equally. The extended family includes a husband and his wife or wives, the husband's parents if they are still living, his sons and their wives and children, and his unmarried sons and daughters. Not until the father dies do his sons split away from this unit and head their own extended households.

Traditionally, parents arrange marriages, which take place within the extended family. Unions between a father's daughter and his brother's son (first cousins) are considered ideal. In this way, the daughter will already know the family she will be living with. Also the bride-price (the gift from the groom to the bride) can be lower because the marriage is contained within the family unit.

With the industrialization of Kuwait, Bedouin herders have

given up their nomadic lifestyle in favor of the steady, paid employment in Kuwait's cities. These changes have decreased the size of families living together because of the limited space in urban areas. Yet the extended family remains the organizing principle in Kuwait. Even households made up of only parents and their children tend to live near relatives.

Kuwaiti women exercise more social independence than women in most Gulf Arab countries. Unlike Saudi Arabian women, for instance, Kuwaiti women are allowed to vote, drive cars, and go out in public without veils. Traditional values still limit their freedom, however, especially when compared to Western lifestyles. Women may attend school and seek employment, but they often are segregated from men in these activities.

Education presents Kuwaiti women with options besides those of wife and mother. Equal numbers of girls and boys have entered primary schools in recent years. The number of women in the workforce has increased steadily since the 1960s. Many women in Kuwait hold advanced degrees and have careers in medicine, industry, and

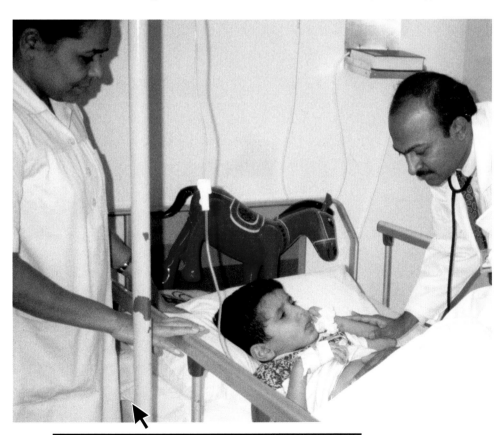

A **woman on the staff of a hospital cancer ward in Kuwait** discusses care for this child with a doctor.

other fields. But the majority of these female workers come from other nations. This trend suggests that Kuwaiti women have not changed their lifestyle as much as noncitizen women living in Kuwait.

Although women traditionally have not had a direct political voice in Kuwaiti society, they have frequently influenced the decisions of male members of their family. Women began to organize formally in the 1960s when they established the Women's Social and Cultural Association. The activities of women have been confined largely to social welfare and humanitarian programs. But during the first Persian Gulf war, women served alongside men as resistance fighters and as translators with the coalition forces. After the war, they began to demand more participation in their country's governance. When the National Assembly voted to give women citizens the right to vote in 2005, it showed that attitudes toward women have begun to change in Kuwait. But traditions often continue as they have for centuries.

Health Care

The rapid increase of income from the oil industry has enabled Kuwait to greatly improve its health services since the 1950s. An infant mortality rate (IMR) that stood at over 120 deaths for every 1,000 live births in the early twentieth century dropped to 10 deaths per 1,000 in 2006. This measurement is a good indicator of the overall health of a nation. In the region, Israel has the lowest IMR of 5 deaths out of 1,000 infants, while Iraq's is the highest with an IMR of 94 per 1,000.

Kuwait's life expectancy likewise improved dramatically. Kuwaitis can expect to live an average of 78 years (79 for women, 77 for men). This is the same as the U.S. average. Only Israel's life expectancy average of 80 years is higher in the Middle East, while Iraq's life expectancy of 59 years is the lowest.

All residents—citizens and noncitizens alike—receive free medical care, funded by the state. Improved health services have eliminated many threats, such as smallpox, that previously plagued the country. The main causes of death are ailments that are common to many industrialized nations—such as heart disease, cancer, and traffic accidents. The rate of HIV/AIDS is 0.12 percent, average for the region. About one-third of the nation's Kuwaiti doctors are women.

In addition to its health-care system, Kuwait also provides citizens with a wide range of welfare programs. The system makes payments to the disabled, the elderly, families of students, widows,

In the early 2000s, **Kuwaiti hospitals** such as this one have dozens of empty beds. Kuwait prepared for retaliation from Iraq for Kuwait's support for the U.S.-led war in Iraq, also called the second Persian Gulf war or Operation Iraqi Freedom. But Iraq has not attacked.

unmarried women over the age of eighteen, orphans, the poor, and families of prisoners.

⊙ Education

Until modern times, education in Kuwait almost entirely consisted of Islamic religious instruction. Boys memorized the Quran (Islam's holy book), and some learned basic reading and writing. Girls were considered mentally inferior and learned how to run households. Primary schools began to operate schools in Kuwait in 1912. Girls' education began in 1937.

In the modern era, Kuwait has made education one of its biggest concerns. The government channels large sums of money, almost 9 percent of its budget, into schools. Kuwait's educational system is therefore one of the best in the Middle East.

Public schools are free from kindergarten through college. All children aged six to fourteen must attend school, by law. Enrollment in primary school is 85 percent. Many children start kindergarten when they are four and continue their schooling until they are eighteen. Instructors in state-run schools teach in Arabic, the official language of Kuwait. Students aged ten and older learn English as a second language. More than one hundred private

Kuwaiti women's rights activists carry signs in Engish as well as Arabic at a gathering in front of the Kuwait National Assembly building in the early 2000s. In Kuwait students learn English as a second language beginning at the age of ten. It is a practical choice since not only the foreign press but many of Kuwait's newest noncitizens have also studied English.

Kuwait University reports it has more than 120 academic departments and more than one thousand faculty members.

schools exist in Kuwait, attended mostly by noncitizens who often cannot gain admission to state-run institutions.

The government covers the cost of books, uniforms, meals, and transportation. In addition, parents receive an allowance to help cover educational expenses. The state also offers scholarships to college students who study abroad. Kuwait provides scholarships for Arab, Asian, and African students to come and study at Kuwait University. Kuwait University was founded in 1966. More than twenty thousand students attend the university.

 Visit www.vgsbooks.com for links to websites with the latest population statistics and information about family life, health care, education, and the languages spoken in Kuwait.

In keeping with strict interpretation of Muslim codes of modesty, girls and women attend school separately from boys and men. Women receive training in home economics, maternity, and child care. They may also prepare for jobs—as secretaries and teachers, for example—that are traditionally accepted for women. Although women are not encouraged to enroll in mechanical or engineering programs or to study abroad, they are gaining acceptance as medical doctors. In 1996 lawmakers passed laws to ensure that college students' behavior, clothing, and activities observed Sharia. It outlaws gambling, drinking, sex outside of marriage, and other matters of personal behavior.

The efforts to spread literacy have been very successful. In 1957 less than 45 percent of the population could read. In the twenty-first century, 83 percent of the adult population is literate. Among

Young women attend a high school chemistry class in Kuwait City. Some cover their heads in the traditional Muslim way. Other equally devout Muslim women consider covering their heads old fashioned.

people under twenty-four years old, literacy has reached 93 percent. About the same percentage of young women and young men can read and write.

Language

Arabic, Kuwait's official language, exists in three forms. Classical Arabic is the literary language of the Quran. Modern Standard Arabic (MSA) comes from Classical Arabic. MSA is a written language used in the press and in literature across the Arab world. It is also the spoken language of the media—broadcasters on the all-Arab TV station Al Jazeera, for instance, speak MSA. The third form, everyday Arabic, varies widely among the many Arab-speaking nations.

Most Arabic last names begin with one of several words that indicates a family relationship. *Bin* or *ibn* means "son of." *Bani* is the plural, "sons of," and is used to name a tribe with a common ancestor. *Bint* means "daughter of." *Al* denotes an extended family or clan, such as al-Sabah, the Sabah family.

The Arabic alphabet has several sounds that are not found in the English language. This makes exact transliteration (changing one alphabet's letters into another's) impossible. Many different ways exist to transliterate Arabic into English. For instance, the name of Islam's prophet can be spelled several different ways in English, including Mahomet, Mohammid, Muhammad, and Muhammed.

In Kuwait many people of all backgrounds also speak English. Immigrants speak the languages of their homelands. People from Iran speak Persian, also called Farsi, not Arabic.

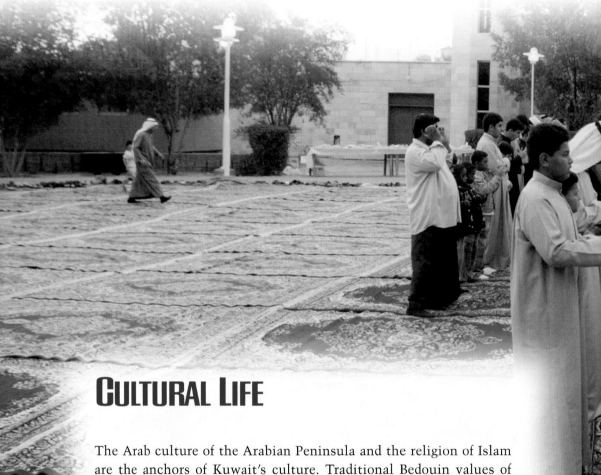

CULTURAL LIFE

The Arab culture of the Arabian Peninsula and the religion of Islam are the anchors of Kuwait's culture. Traditional Bedouin values of bravery, generosity, and hospitality remain shared values in Kuwait. The ravages of the Iraqi occupation increased Kuwaitis' awareness of the value of traditional culture. The many immigrants from other countries also bring their cultures to Kuwait. This diversity enriches the flavors of the country's cuisine and music. Western television and movies influence young Kuwaitis though. The nation is more socially open and free to exchange ideas than most of the other Persian Gulf states.

◉ Religion

Islam is the official religion of Kuwait. Almost all Kuwaiti citizens are Muslims. Eighty-five percent of noncitizens are also Muslims. The other 15 percent of non-Kuwaitis follow other faiths. These include Hinduism (the main religion of India since 1500 B.C.), Parsi

(from an ancient Iranian religion), and Christian groups such as Protestants and Roman Catholics.

Islam is a monotheistic religion that shares roots with Judaism and Christianity. Muslims accept the prophet Muhammad as the last and greatest spiritual spokesperson of Allah, completing the messages of Abraham, Moses, and Jesus. They believe that Muhammad received the word of God through the angel Gabriel. These messages are recorded in the Quran. Muslims look to the Quran for political and social guidance as well as spiritual inspiration. They also respect the hadith, also called the Traditions of the Prophet. This is the written collection of Muhammad's sayings and deeds.

Islam means "submission" and is related to the Arabic word for "peace." Submission to the will of Allah is the guiding principle of Islam. The Quran teaches it is Allah's will that people should act honestly, chastely, generously, respectfully, and fairly.

Muslims follow five main duties of their faith, known as the five pillars of Islam. The first and central pillar is declaring faith in one god, Allah, and his prophet Muhammad. The other four pillars are praying five times daily, fasting during the holy month of Ramadan, giving alms (charity), and making the pilgrimage to the holy city of Mecca, Saudi Arabia, at least once in a lifetime, if possible.

The Muslim population in Kuwait is about 80 percent Sunni and 20 percent Shiite. (The ruling Sabah family is/are Sunni.) The two groups represent the two major Islamic sects that arose after the death of Muhammad in 632. At that time, Sunnis agreed to elect religious leaders. Shiites, however, maintained that only descendants of Muhammad could lead the Islamic community.

Most of the Shiites in Kuwait originally came from Iran, where Shiites make up a majority of the population. Some of the Shiites living in Kuwait arrived before the 1920s and thus qualify for Kuwaiti citizenship. When Shiites in Iran gained power following the 1979 Islamic Revolution, they began to encourage aggressive, anti-Sunni sentiments among Shiites in Kuwait. Consequently, Sunnis in Kuwait feared that the Shiites might disrupt Kuwaiti society. In 1988 Kuwait expelled several thousand Shiites after terrorist bombings.

Another religious force exists among Kuwait's Sunnis: fundamentalists, or conservatives who want strict observance of Islam's basic, fundamental principles and ideas. This group believes that the rapid modernization of the nation and Western influences have worn away Islamic morals. The most extreme of the country's fundamentalists reject all forms of modernization. Instead, they want public and private standards of behavior to return to the way they were during the life of Muhammad. Some extremists are willing to use violence to achieve their goals.

Many Indians and other south Asians are followers of Hinduism, the world's oldest major religion still

TINY QURANS

The Tareq Rajab Museum in Kuwait City has several tiny but perfectly handwritten Qurans. Because Muslims consider the Quran to be the word of Allah, the book has a special place in Islamic art. Over the centuries, Muslim artists have created Qurans that are among the world's most beautiful works of art. Islam forbids pictures of Allah and discourages depictions of humans. Therefore, many artists concentrated on developing decorative styles of handwriting. One style was written in miniature but very clear script. This was first used for messages sent by pigeon, but eventually artists created popular, tiny Qurans using this script.

Kuwaiti children enjoy carnival rides during the Muslim holiday Eid al-Fitr. This two-day festival marks the end of Ramadan.

existing. The concepts of karma and reincarnation are its central beliefs. Karma is the belief that every action causes a good or bad reaction. Reincarnation is the belief that each being is born over and over again. The karma of previous lives shapes the next lifetime. Eventually, good actions can free the believer from this cycle of death and rebirth. Hindus worship many deities, or gods and goddesses, and build elaborate temples to them. The many deities are representations of different aspects of Brahman, or the Supreme God. The four Veda are the sacred books of Hinduism.

A smaller number of Indian Kuwaitis practice the Parsi religion. This is a sect of the Zoroastrian religion established by the Persian prophet Zoroaster, probably in the 1200s B.C. Modern Parsis are descended from immigrants who fled to India in the A.D. 900s escaping religious persecution in Persia. Their name means "the Persians." They believe in one god, called Ahura Mazda, the creator of all that is good. Their religious worship centers on fire as a symbol of purity. A sacred fire burns in temples, and nonbelievers cannot enter the fire temples. The Parsi holy book is called the Avesta. It teaches high ideals of good thoughts, good words, and good deeds.

Holidays

The most important holy time in Kuwait is the Islamic month of Ramadan, the anniversary of when Allah first called Muhammad to be his prophet. During this month, observant Muslims do not drink, eat, or smoke during daylight hours. Places of work shorten their hours. At night,

THE HEGIRA CALENDAR

For everyday purposes, Kuwaitis follow the same Gregorian calendar used in the West. But Islamic holidays follow a lunar (moon phases) calendar. The calendar dates from A.D. 622. In this year, the prophet Muhammad fled from Mecca to escape being murdered by his enemies. This event is called the hegira, which means "flight." Islamic dates are followed with the letters A.H. They stand for Anno Hejiri, which means "years after the flight." The year A.D. 2000 corresponds to the year 1420 A.H. This hegira calendar is eleven days shorter than the solar year. Therefore, the seasons of religious holidays vary.

cities are lively as many people stay awake to eat and socialize with friends and family. Ramadan ends with two days of celebration, called Eid al-Fitr. The other main Islamic holidays are Muharram 1, the first day of the Muslim year; Mouloud, the prophet Muhammad's birthday; and Eid al-Adha, or the Feast of the Sacrifice. On this holiday, the Muslims who can afford it sacrifice a sheep and share the meat with the poor. Eid al-Adha takes place after the time of the pilgrimage to Mecca, called the hajj. Friday is the holy day of the week for Muslims. On Fridays many people go to their local mosque to pray and listen to a religious teacher. Thursday and Friday is the weekend in Kuwait.

Kuwait has several secular holidays. New Year's Day is January 1. Liberation Day on February 26 celebrates the end of seven months of Iraqi occupation in 1991. The Hala February festival takes place every spring when flowers and the arrival of migratory birds transform the desert. People take picnics to the desert during this season.

◐ Social Networks

Kuwaitis have no organized form of political parties or trade unions. Nevertheless, Kuwaiti citizens have informal ways to express their concerns to National Assembly representatives or to members of the ruling Sabah family. This extended family has more than one thousand members. Communication is often done through a relative or a friend who knows someone with influence.

Decision makers can also be reached directly at a *diwan* (Arabic for "gathering," *diwaniya* is the plural), or a private club for men. Diwaniya provide a framework for solving disputes and for reaching agreements on various matters. Members sit on the floor in a loose circle, drink tea and coffee, and talk. Discussions take place in a specific manner. In this way, connections are made and favors may be

In Kuwait **serving coffee** or tea is an important expression of hospitality.

asked indirectly and discreetly through a friend. Members arrange appointments, settle contracts, make introductions, and offer jobs—all in subtle ways. Businessmen and important officials sometimes publish the times of their diwaniya in the newspaper so members of the public can attend.

Art and Architecture

Kuwait's traditional arts and crafts include wood carving, leatherwork, textile arts, palm frond basketry, jewelry making, and traditional boat-building. Bedouin art represents Kuwait's best-known folk art. Because nomads were always on the move, Bedouin art is portable. Some

Kuwaitis have revived Bedouin *sadu*, or weaving, traditionally done by women on a small loom. Sadu includes brightly colored carpets, bridles, saddlebags, and pillows. Bedouin jewelers create beautiful silver bracelets, belts, forehead bands, and necklaces.

The National Council for Culture, Arts, and Literature has led a revival of Kuwait's artistic traditions since 1974. The council organizes a cultural festival every year. Known as the Qurain Festival, it features artists and musicians from Kuwait and other countries.

Modern styles of painting and sculpture have only recently developed in Kuwait, in part because Islam discourages representations of human images. One artist who has gained prominence is the sculptor Sami Mohammed. His statue in Kuwait City's Safat Square is a tribute to the nation's seafaring past. It is constructed in the shape of a huge open oyster with a pearl inside the shell.

Oil wealth has given the country the opportunity to create world-class modern architecture. After the discovery of oil, architecture took a modern turn, with an emphasis on technology and industry. After the 1991 war, architects began to use traditional elements mixed with modern styles.

At **Bayt al-Sadu, or al-Sadu House,** in Kuwait City, a photograph of a woman demonstrating sadu, or Bedouin weaving, is displayed among examples of the craft. The building houses a weaving cooperative owned and operated by the weavers themselves.

The 32,300 sq. ft. (3,000 sq. m) roof of the **Kuwait National Assembly building** also covers a public square. Its architect Jorn Utzon also designed the famous Sydney Opera House in Sydney, Australia.

Kuwait's architecture is a combination of old and new, simple and elegant. The blend can be seen in the swooping white roofs of the National Assembly building, designed to look like Bedouin tents. In the past, Kuwaitis who were not nomads built simple mud-brick houses. Mosaics (designs made with tiny tiles) and ornamental patterns decorated the structures. Typically, a house was built around a central courtyard.

Over the centuries, Arab artists developed complex geometrical styles, often based on mathematical formulas or floral patterns. These designs decorate surfaces of buildings. Kuwait City's Grand Mosque is decorated inside and out with Islamic designs. Religious verses in calligraphy (decorative script) also adorn the mosque and other buildings.

Music and Dance

Both traditional and modern music is popular in Kuwait. Chanteys (sailors' songs) are one of the most distinctive Kuwaiti songs from the past. The words and rhythms of chanteys accompanied tasks done on pearling ships. Traders also brought music from India and East Africa to influence Kuwaiti styles. *Mawleds,* chants about Muhammad's life, are recited on religious holidays.

Kuwaiti musicians who perform a blues style of music known as *sawt* are popular around the Gulf region. Modern sawt performers includes Shadi al Khaleej, known as the Bird Song of the Gulf. Popular sawt musicians mix Western pop and techno in their music.

Bedouin culture includes dances such as the *ardah* at festivals and marriages. Drums and tambourines accompany male ardah dancers, who use swords to demonstrate their agility and bravery. Women perform other dances at family and social events. Modern folklore troupes perform popular songs and dances at gatherings. Traditional Bedouin instruments include the lutelike oud, small drums called *al-mirwas*, and the bagpipe *al-habban*. The *rubabah* is a single-stringed instrument made of thin leather stretched round a wooden frame.

◉ Literature and Film

The spoken word was the center of Kuwait's literary culture for generations. The Bedouin and coastal people have a long history of poetry and folklore memorized and passed on by word of mouth. Thousands of tales from the desert and the sea, riddles, and proverbs (wisdom sayings) were the literature of a nomadic culture. In 1956 the Folklore Preservation Center began to collect disappearing Kuwaiti folklore. Performers sing songs based on these tales. With literacy on the rise only in recent generations, modern Kuwaiti literature is in a development stage. Few English translations are available.

The first movie filmed in Kuwait was a 1930 documentary about sailing, *Sons of Sinbad*. Kuwait's first feature film, *Bas Ya Bahar* (known abroad as *Sea and Silence*), was released in 1972. Directed by Khaled el Seddik, the film won nine international film festival awards. It tells the story of a poor son of a pearl diver crippled by a shark attack. The father tries to protect his son by forbidding him to become a pearl diver. When the young man falls in love and needs money to marry, he goes to sea anyway. The director went on to make *al-Zain Wedding* (1982) and *Shaheen* (1986). Kuwait has produced a number of films popular in the Arab world. Jobs in video production, television, and advertising are popular among young Kuwaitis.

◉ Sports and Recreation

Soccer, called football outside of the United States, is the most popular sport in Kuwait. It is played at schools and sports clubs throughout the country. The national soccer team has won both Arab and international competitions.

Kuwaitis have an international reputation in horse racing. Riders also compete in long-distance endurance races. Camel racing is a major sport with a long history. Though Islam outlaws gambling, large amounts of money are spent on unofficial bets on the winners. Car racing is also very popular.

Kuwait's location on the Persian Gulf offers great opportunities for sea sports. Some areas of the Gulf, however, continue to be unsafe due to unexploded mines remaining from the first Gulf war. Clubs around Kuwait City provide equipment for windsurfing, water-skiing, scuba diving, and yachting. Although Kuwait has many excellent beaches, people usually swim in pools because jellyfish in the Gulf waters are a hazard during much of the year. The government owns and runs several sports clubs, which have facilities for swimming, tennis, and other activities.

Nomadic life holds a charm for modern city dwellers, and Kuwaitis like to go camping to enjoy the desert of their ancestors. Black, camel-hair Bedouin tents have been replaced by modern tents with electricity, hot water, and other comforts.

FALCONRY

Falconry is an ancient pastime of Bedouin sheikhs. Some modern Kuwaitis still practice the sport. They breed falcons or catch them along the Gulf coast when the birds come through on their annual migration. Falconers teach the highly intelligent birds to catch and return prey to them. The falcons hunt desert hares and the rare desert bird, the houbara bustard. Both wild falcons and their desert prey have become scarce. The popularity of the sport has led to conservation efforts to protect the animals and their environment.

A **falconer** wears a thick glove to protect his hand from the falcon's talons.

Vegetables and vendors compete for attention in this souk in Kuwait City.

Food

Kuwait's cuisine reflects the country's history, its traders and immigrants, and its legacy of the desert and the sea. The cuisine is a unique blend of Bedouin, Persian, Indian, and Middle Eastern influences. Kuwait's diverse population ensures that Arabian, Western, Indian, and Asian foods are found in homes, restaurants, and shops.

Traditional dishes feature lamb, fish, and seafood such as shrimp. Bedouin meals were cooked in a single pot over an open fire. Cooks simmered meat, fish, and vegetables with rice or wheat and spices. *Baharat* is a common spice mix of cardamom, cinnamon, cloves, coriander, cumin, ginger, nutmeg, black pepper, and paprika.

Loomi is a common ingredient in Kuwaiti dishes. Loomi is dried and blackened lime, which has a strong and unusual flavor. It is hard to find in the United States, and grated lime peel is a suggested substitute.

Kuwait shares many dishes with other Arab nations. *Laban*, or yogurt, is a standard food. Tabbouleh is a salad of bulgur (grains of coarse-ground wheat), chopped parsley, mint, tomatoes, and onion. Hummus is a dip made of ground chickpeas and sesame-seed paste. Pita bread is a soft, flat bread. *Shawarma* sandwiches wrap roasted lamb, beef, or chicken in pita bread. The meat is topped with fresh vegetables and a sauce. Islam forbids eating pork or drinking alcohol. Coffee is an important part of a meal, especially when guests are present. Offering and receiving coffee is part of the desert tradition of giving hospitality to all comers.

HUMMUS

This dip of ground chickpeas and tahini (sesame-seed paste) is a classic in the Arab world. Add more or less lemon juice and garlic, depending on your taste. Hummus is also good with sliced fresh vegetables such as cucumbers and tomatoes, which grow in Kuwait.

2 15-oz. cans chickpeas

½ cup lemon juice

⅓ cup tahini (sesame-seed paste)

½ tablespoon salt

2 or 3 cloves of garlic, chopped

olive oil

parsley sprigs for garnish

pita bread, cut into pieces for dipping

1. Drain and rinse the chickpeas. Set aside a few for garnish, and put the rest in a blender or food processor. Add lemon juice, tahini, salt, and garlic. Process until smooth.
2. Transfer to serving bowl. Drizzle olive oil on top of hummus. Garnish with reserved chickpeas and parsley sprigs.
3. Serve with pita bread.

Serves 6.

THE ECONOMY

Kuwait plays a far greater role in the world's economy than most countries of such a small size and population. This desert country ranks as one of the main producers of oil in the world. Scientists estimate Kuwait's proven reserves of crude oil to be about 10 percent of the earth's total reserves. More than 1,500 wells produce oil in Kuwait. The government receives a majority of its revenues from the export of oil and its by-products.

Kuwait's gross national product, or GNP (the amount of goods and services produced in a country per year, including foreign income), is among the world's highest. Careful planning and investment have increased Kuwait's output of oil, power, and water. These resources are necessary for industry and to provide for the population.

Experts predict that Kuwait's known oil reserves will last more than two hundred years. But dependency on one industry does not create a stable economy. Furthermore, the price of oil on the world market varies, adding to economic instability. Therefore, Kuwait works to

attract new industries to diversify its economy. Looking to the future when the oil runs out, it also channels 10 percent of its oil earnings into a Future Generations Fund. This money is carefully invested around the world.

With the 2003 removal of the threat of Saddam Hussein's regime, Kuwait began to invest in large infrastructure projects. Construction began on more tourist attractions, oil refineries, oil tankers, electric power stations, and water distillation plants. Many international companies also set up offices in Kuwait, bringing additional business to the country. These developments should lead to new sources of income and employment.

Oil and Energy

The oil sector includes mining, manufacturing, construction, and power industries. The sector provides 60.5 percent of Kuwait's gross domestic product (GDP, the value of goods and services produced in a

THE SEVEN SISTERS

The Seven Sisters is the nickname of the seven major oil companies that once controlled most of the world's petroleum business. The companies were Shell, Exxon, Mobil, Chevron, Texaco, Gulf, and British Petroleum (BP). Until the rise of OPEC and Arab states' control of their own resources, these Western-owned companies dominated world oil production, refinement, and distribution. Well organized and hugely wealthy, the seven companies went through numerous mergers and name changes. The remaining companies are ExxonMobil, Chevron, Shell, and BP.

country in a year, not counting foreign income). It funds almost all government spending. Industry employs only 17 percent of the workforce, however, as the work is largely mechanized. Petroleum production is the most important industry in the country.

Significant deposits of natural gas are found along with petroleum deposits. Gas provides energy to run electrical plants. Kuwaitis use a large amount of electricity because they rely on air-conditioning and desalinated water.

The Kuwaiti government owns and controls almost all aspects of its oil industry, from production to transportation and marketing. The government uses its earnings from oil to build modern cities and to provide social services. It also invests billions of dollars abroad and earns significant amounts from careful investments. But because the price and demand for oil are unpredictable, Kuwait is working to develop a wide variety of profitable industries. Some of these businesses will focus on refining crude oil into other products. The government also plans to sell some of its oil-related companies to foreign investors.

At the Burgan Oil Field, saltwater is separated from oil in these tanks.

Founded in 1980, the Kuwait Petroleum Corporation (KPC) plays a key role in managing the entire oil sector. KPC ranks among the world's major international oil companies, once known as the Seven Sisters. In 1998 two major international oil companies, British Petroleum and the American oil company Amoco, merged. In 2001 the company took the name BP. KPC owns 10 percent of BP.

Kuwait Oil Company is responsible for exploration, drilling, and processing of oil in the nation. Other organizations have taken over secondary tasks. Kuwait National Petroleum Company controls refining, local marketing, and converting gas into liquid fuel. Kuwait Oil Tanker Company organizes the transport of crude oil, liquid gas, and oil products to Kuwait's world markets. Exploration activities continue both on land and under the ocean. Kuwait is also the first OPEC member to explore for oil outside its own borders.

Manufacturing and Trade

Manufacturing is a small part of the industrial sector. Petroleum refineries that process crude oil into petroleum products make up three-fourths of manufacturing activities. Modern factories in Kuwait also produce cement, bricks, paints, batteries, and woolen blankets. Many factories operate at ash-Shuaybah, ash-Shuwaykh, and al-Ahmadi. These industrial areas host ship repair yards, desalination plants, and plants for making fertilizers, cement, and petrochemicals. Officials are working to develop Kuwait's petrochemical production. It is expanding beyond producing low-value products such as ammonia into high-value products such as ethylene and polyethylene.

Kuwait's lack of raw materials other than petroleum slows the growth of industry. Using profits from oil, Kuwaiti leaders have encouraged industrialization within the country. The government provides start-up money, trains workers, and conducts technical studies to help industries. It also offers tax breaks and loans at low interest rates to businesspeople. It pays part of the cost of electricity and water too.

Imports come from Japan, the United States, and Germany. Kuwait has a very favorable balance of trade—the difference between money earned from exports and money spent on imports. Major imports include machinery, manufactured goods, food, and raw materials except for fuels.

Before the first Gulf war, Kuwait had $100 billion in overseas investments. The nation had to spend half of that to pay for the war and for rebuilding afterward. Since then it has slowly built up its investments again.

Oil provides 95 percent of Kuwait's export income (money from selling to other countries). Oil brings in billions of dollars annually. Kuwait exports more than 60 percent of its oil to Asian countries including Japan, India, and South Korea. Kuwait also ships oil to Europe and the United States. The country's main export port is Mina al-Ahmadi. This port can handle the largest oil tankers in the world. Besides oil, Kuwait exports very little. Factories manufacture fertilizer and process seafood for export. Pearl fishing continues on a reduced scale, but Japan supplies most of the world demand for the gems.

Services and Tourism

The service sector of a country's economy provides services rather than producing goods. It includes jobs in government, health care, education, retail trade, banking, and tourism. Service work contributes

Pricey travel souvenirs are available in Kuwait City's gold souks.

39 percent of Kuwait's GDP and employs 82 percent of the working population. Because the oil industry requires only a small number of workers, the government has set aside sizable funds to provide jobs in the service sector.

The government employs most of the Kuwaiti-citizen workforce. Guaranteed employment for citizens is a heavy burden on government spending. The government spends a large amount of the annual budget on salaries. Public administration and jobs in construction, trade, restaurants, and hotels employ the largest percentages of noncitizens.

Foreign visitors bring Kuwait more than $320 million yearly. Most visitors are business travelers from Saudi Arabia, India, and Egypt. For pleasure travelers, attractions include the Kuwait City Water Towers leisure complex and Entertainment City, modeled after Disneyland. Recreational activities include water sports such as sailing.

The country outlined a tourism development plan in 2004. Boosting tourism will diversify the economy and create new jobs. The twenty-year plan includes new hotels and resorts, as well as environmental and scientific exhibits. It is designed to attract both foreigners and Kuwaitis to travel in the country. Most Kuwaitis leave the country to vacation abroad. But studies show that many would vacation in their own country if better tourism facilities were available. Billion-dollar plans are under way to develop Faylakah Island, home to Kuwait's main archaeological site, and Bubiyan Island, with its white sand beaches and coral reefs.

Agriculture and Fishing

Because of Kuwait's intense heat and vast desert, only 1 percent of its land is suitable for farming. Agriculture accounts for 0.5 percent of the nation's GDP. The sector employs 1 percent of the workforce. The Kuwaiti government has sought to increase agricultural output by irrigating the desert and by starting an experimental farm that produces eggs and milk and that raises poultry. This farm also conducts research on hydroponic farming—a method of growing crops in greenhouses without using soil.

Kuwait's main crops are tomatoes, potatoes, cucumbers, eggplants, melons, dates, and onions. Very little grain is grown, since it requires a lot of water. Farmers raise cattle, goats, camels, and sheep for meat and milk. Sheep also provide sheepskins and wool. The nation must import much of its food. Food makes up 14 percent of the country's imports.

One of Kuwait's oldest economic activities is fishing. However, pollution from the oil industry and from desalinization plants has harmed fish and shrimp habitats. Shrimp are an important product in Kuwait. Workers freeze and export shrimp to Europe and the United States.

Boatbuilding facilities and seafood packing plants contribute to the fishing industry. Pearl fishing off the country's coast is a source of income for some Kuwaitis, and others fashion the pearls into jewelry.

Transportation and Communications

Kuwait has a network of more than 2,765 miles (4,450 km) of roads. More than one out of three people in Kuwait owns a car, an example of the nation's high standard of living. International highways link Kuwait to Iraq and to Saudi Arabia. There are no railways in Kuwait. At a cost of more than $600 million, Kuwait International Airport is expanding its facilities. Kuwait Airways operates regional and international flights. al-Jazeera Airways began in 2005 to operate low-cost flights to other Middle Eastern countries. Three commercial ports serve Kuwait.

The journalistic press in Kuwait is much more open than in many other Arab countries. However, the government's fear of political unrest has occasionally led to press censorship. In 1995 the Constitutional Court gave the government the right to censor newspapers. Laws also forbid the press from insulting Allah and his prophet, Muhammad. Lawbreakers face prison sentences. Journalists also do not criticize the royal family in print.

Eight daily and twenty weekly newspapers are published in Kuwait. Most are in Arabic, but the daily *Arab Times* and the *Kuwait Times* are in English. Daily newspapers also arrive from abroad by air each morning. The Ministry of Information issues newspaper publishers' licenses. The ministry censors newspapers, magazines, books, and movies to prevent morally offensive material. The government press publishes books, periodicals, pamphlets, and laws.

Satellite dishes bring television news and shows from all over the world to Kuwait. During the Gulf wars, many Kuwaiti viewers relied on the U.S news channel Cable News Network (CNN) more than on local news for coverage of events.

Kuwait's first local radio broadcasting station opened in 1951. It grew during the country's rapid expansion and can be heard in the United States. State-run radio and television stations exist side-by-side with privately owned media businesses. More than 1 million televisions and many more radios are in use.

Kuwait's privately owned communications company offers an excellent telephone network. Modern telecommunications facilities connect Kuwait with the rest of the world. More than 1.5 million Kuwaitis subscribe to cell phones. More than half a million use the Internet.

For links to the latest news from Kuwait and more information about its economy, go to www.vgsbooks.com.

The Future

The removal of Saddam Hussein's regime in 2003 eliminated one of the threats to stability in Kuwait. Terrorism and regional tensions still threaten the Middle East, however. Because Kuwait is a small country surrounded by powerful neighbors, much of the nation's future depends upon a lasting peace in the region.

While oil production is Kuwait's economic mainstay, the government wants to decrease the country's dependency on this resource. Officials seek to attract foreign companies to diversify the economy. In addition, the government is privatizing many of its industries, selling some parts to both foreign and Kuwaiti investors.

Kuwait is also striving to establish a more democratic system of government. Women citizens voted for the first time in the 2006 parliamentary elections. The National Assembly is often in opposition to the ruling Sabah government, a stance that many Kuwaitis support. But because the emir has the authority to dissolve the assembly at any time, Kuwait's political future remains uncertain. Sheikh Sabah became emir in early 2006. He faces the challenge of balancing the forces of Islamic moderates and extremists in the government, in the country, and in the larger Middle East. With Kuwait's wealth and high level of education and social services, the nation is well positioned to face these challenges.

Timeline

5000 B.C. People of the al-Ubaid culture live in the area of present-day Kuwait.

4000–2000 The Dilmun civilization arises. Humans cultivate date palms on the Arabian Peninsula. Dilmun controls the trade route to India.

2000–1800 The Dilmun culture declines. Piracy flourishes in the Persian Gulf.

600 The Babylonians and later the Persians (in present-day Iran) control Dilmun.

330s Greeks establish a colony on the island of Faylakah, which they call Ikaros.

200 Herders domesticate wild camels on the Arabian Peninsula.

A.D. 313 The Roman Empire adopts Christianity, influencing Roman-held lands around the Persian Gulf.

MID-600s Kuwait comes under Muslim rule. The Bedouin inhabit the desert.

1500s European powers compete for control of the Persian Gulf.

1722 The Bani Utub settle at a small town they call Kuwait.

1756 Sabah bin Jaber is elected to be the first sheikh (leader) of the Bani Utub.

1760s Most of Kuwait's population of 10,000 work as pearlers, fishers, boat makers, and traders along Kuwait's coast.

1775 The British move businesses from Iraq to Kuwait City, establishing a British presence in Kuwait.

LATE 1700s British forces help defend Kuwait against Saudi Arabian Wahhabis.

1800s British control of Kuwait keeps the Ottoman Turks and the Persians across the Gulf from successfully challenging Kuwaiti control of the major trade routes.

1866 Sheikh Abdallah al-Sabah begins his reign and accepts Ottoman control.

1899 Kuwait becomes a protectorate (a dependent state) of Great Britain.

1913 Kuwait and the Ottoman Empire define Kuwait's northern border with Iraq.

1920 Kuwaitis defeat Saudi Arabian forces at al-Jahrah.

1934 Sheikh Ahmad al-Sabah grants the Kuwait Oil Company permission to explore for oil.

1937 Girls' education in Kuwait begins.

1938 Drillers discover oil under Kuwait's desert at Burgan Oil Field.

1946 Export of oil begins. Foreign companies control the oil industry.

1948   Kuwait disapproves of the establishment of the nation of
Israel. Many Palestinians immigrate to Kuwait.

1951   Kuwait's emir (ruler) gains equal shares in Kuwait Oil Company profits.
He uses the money to fund education and other public works programs.

1961   Kuwait achieves full independence on June 19.

1962   Kuwait adopts a constitution. Government programs aim to distribute oil
wealth fairly among Kuwaiti citizens.

1969   Kuwait and Saudi Arabia split the Neutral Zone—subsequently renamed the Divided
Zone. Each country administers its own portion but shares the oil resources.

1972   Kuwait's first feature film, *Bas Ya Bahar* (*Sea and Silence*), is released.

1973   After the 1973 Arab-Israeli War, Kuwait and other Arab oil-producing countries cut
back shipments of oil to countries that supported Israel and increase the price of oil.

1977   Jaber al-Ahmad al-Sabah becomes the thirteenth emir from the Sabah family.

1980   The Iran-Iraq War begins. Kuwait is neutral but gives Iraq loans and aid.

1985   A pro-Iranian Islamist militant (a violent supporter of Islam as a political force) tries
and fails to assassinate Emir Sheikh Jaber.

1987   After Iran threatens Kuwait's shipping, the United States agrees to escort Kuwaiti
ships through the Persian Gulf.

1988   The Iran-Iraq War ends with a huge loss of life and property damage on both sides.

1990   Iraq's dictator, Saddam Hussein, orders the takeover of Kuwait on August 2.

1991   On February 26, Kuwaiti and allied soldiers enter Kuwait City, ending Iraq's occupation
of Kuwait. Iraqi soldiers set fire to oil wells and release oil into the Persian Gulf.

1993   Most repairs of Kuwait's war damage are completed by the end of the year.

1995   The Constitutional Court allows the government to censor newspapers.

1996   The government gives the right to vote to men who have lived in Kuwait for thirty
years. Kuwait University opens.

2001   Kuwait condemns the September 11 terrorist attacks on the United States.

2003   A U.S.-led coalition invades Iraq and overthrows Saddam Hussein's government.
Kuwait serves as a major partner in this second Persian Gulf war.

2005   Kuwait's lawmakers grant women Kuwaiti citizens the right to vote and
to run for political office. Massouma al-Mubarak becomes the first
woman member of the cabinet.

2006   Sheikh Jaber dies on January 15, 2006. Prime Minister Sabah al-
Ahmad al-Sabah becomes emir.

COUNTRY NAME State of Kuwait

AREA 6,880 square miles (17,818 square kilometers)

MAIN LANDFORMS ash-Shaqaya Peak, Bubiyan Island, Faylakah Island, Kuwait Bay, al-Adan ridge

HIGHEST POINT unnamed location in the southwest, 1,000 feet (305 m) above sea level

MAJOR RIVERS none

ANIMALS Arabian horses, camels, desert hares, falcons, fennecs, flamingos, gerbils, goats, hedgehogs, jackals, jerboas, kestrels, lizards, lobsters, mackerel, mullet, oysters, scorpions, sea turtles, sharks, sheep, shrimp, snakes, Socotra cormorants

CAPITAL CITY Kuwait City (al-Kuwait)

OTHER MAJOR CITIES al-Ahmadi, al-Jahrah, Sabiyah, al-Khiran

OFFICIAL LANGUAGE Arabic

MONETARY UNITY Kuwaiti dinar. 1,000 fils = 1 dinar.

KUWAIT CURRENCY

Kuwait adopted its own currency, the Kuwaiti dinar, in 1961, at independence. Until that time, the country used the Indian rupee. (The British Empire ruled India and introduced the rupee to the Gulf region in the nineteenth century.) Coins come in denominations (amounts) of 1, 5, 10, 20, 50, and 100 fils. Bank notes are issued in denominations of 250 and 500 fils, and 1, 5, 10, and 20 dinars. The government released new designs after the first Persian Gulf war.

Sidebar (vertical): Currency   Fast Facts

Kuwait adopted its national flag when the country gained independence from Britain in 1961. The flag is composed of three horizontal stripes. From top to bottom, they are colored green, white, and red. One vertical black trapezoid on the flagpole side of the flag juts into the stripes. The flag's colors symbolize spring and hope (green), work (white), and the country's glorious past (red). Black symbolizes the people's struggles. Green is also the color of Islam. Kuwait also has a separate national emblem composed of a falcon with open wings around a sailing dhow (boat) on blue and white waves. Its motto is Kuwait Independent.

Kuwait adopted its national anthem in 1978. It is only played on special occasions. Therefore, it is rarely heard in Kuwait. Poet Ahmad Mushari al-Adwani wrote the words, and Ibrahim Nasir al-Soula wrote the music. The National Salute consists of the first stanza of the National Anthem:

Kuwait, Kuwait, Kuwait,
My country,
In peace live, in dignity,
Your face bright,
Your face bright,
Your face bright with majesty,
Kuwait, Kuwait, Kuwait,
My country.

 Hear Kuwait's national anthem. Go to www.vgsbooks.com for a link.

ABDULLAH YACOUB BISHARA (b. 1936) Bishara is a Kuwaiti scholar and a diplomat. He served as Kuwait's ambassador to the United Nations from 1971 to 1981. At that time, he became the secretary-general of the Gulf Cooperation Council (GCC). The GCC is an organization of the Persian Gulf states plus Saudi Arabia. In this position, he oversaw the GCC's progress toward cooperation in areas of economic and security concerns.

VIOLET DICKSON (1896–1991) Born in Gautby, England, Dickson is known for her knowledge of Bedouin life, for her botanical work in Kuwait, and for her contributions to Arab-Western friendship. She moved to Kuwait in 1929 with her husband, Harold Dickson. He was the British government's representative to the emir of Kuwait. When Violet Dickson arrived in Kuwait, only eleven other Europeans lived there. She wrote *The Wild Flowers of Kuwait and Bahrain*, published in 1955. After her husband's death in 1959, she chose to spend the rest of her life in Kuwait. She wrote her memoir, entitled *Forty Years in Kuwait*. In it she records the enormous changes she saw in Kuwait after the discovery of oil in the 1930s. When she was ninety-four, shortly before her death, she left Kuwait to avoid the Iraqi invasion.

JASEM AL-HUWAIDI (b. 1972) Al-Huwaidi was a top-scoring striker on Kuwait's national soccer team from 1992 to 2002. During his career, he scored more than fifty goals in international competitions. Eleven of these goals were in World Cup Qualifiers in 1993, 1997, and 2001.

SAMI MOHAMMED (b. 1943) Mohammed is a famous Kuwaiti sculptor. He was born in Kuwait City. As a boy, he liked to sculpt clay into figures of people and animals. He studied art at the Government Free Atelier. In 1970 he sculpted a starving mother and child group in synthetic marble. The work was called *Hunger*. It expressed his concern for the suffering of humanity. In 1972 he created a large bronze statue of Sheikh Abdallah al-Sabah, a former ruler of Kuwait. Mohammed's statue in Kuwait City's Safat Square celebrates the nation's seafaring past. It portrays a huge open oyster with a pearl inside. Mohammed has taught at Kuwait University and at the Institute for Handicrafts. His art has been seen in 145 exhibits in Kuwait and abroad.

MASSOUMA AL-MUBARAK (b. ca. 1949) In 2005, the same year that Kuwaiti women won the right to vote and hold public office, al-Mubarak became Kuwait's first female cabinet minister. With this breakthrough, Kuwait became the third country in the Gulf Arab region to have a woman minister. Al-Mubarak serves along with fifteen male ministers, some of whom do not approve of her appointment. Her title is planning minister and minister of state for administrative development affairs. Al-Mubarak is a U.S.-educated political science professor, journalist, and woman's rights activist. She is a Shiite

Muslim, a minority in Kuwait. Though she wears the hijab, or head-scarf, she says she considers herself a liberal who looks to the future. Al-Mubarak faces strong opposition among the male-dominated ruling class of Kuwait. In an interview with the press, she said, "The responsibilities are big but I have, Inshala [God willing], the courage to do it."

ABDALLAH AL-SALIM AL-SABAH (1895–1965)

Abdallah was the admired ruler of Kuwait, from 1950 to 1965, who oversaw the transformation of society brought about by the great wealth from oil. Kuwaitis view him as the Father of Kuwait in the age of oil. He guided Kuwait to independence and a constitution. He oversaw the election of the first National Assembly. In a short span of time, he used the country's new riches to establish a complete welfare state. His reign benefited wealthy and powerful Kuwaitis, especially the Sabah family, but it also brought education and health care to all levels of society.

JABER AL-AHMAD AL-SABAH (1926–2006)

Sheikh Jaber became emir of Kuwait in 1977. Jaber was the thirteenth ruler from the Sabah family. When Kuwait gained independence in 1961, Sheikh Jaber became the first finance minister. He helped steer Kuwait at a time when oil wealth was changing the country. In 1965 he was appointed prime minister. Like most other Middle Eastern leaders, Sheikh Jaber weathered a series of regional and domestic challenges. He survived a car bomb assassination attempt in 1985. When Iraq invaded his country during the first Persian Gulf war, Sheikh Jaber created a Kuwaiti government in exile in Saudi Arabia. He gained the support of Kuwait's opposition leaders in return for his agreement to restore the National Assembly. In 1999 Sheikh Jaber tried to give voting rights to Kuwaiti women, but the National Assembly rejected his order. Sheikh Jaber followed the old Gulf tradition of creating alliances with key families by marrying, divorcing, and remarrying women to have up to four wives at a time. He is survived by many children.

MUBARAK BIN SABAH AL-SABAH (1837–1915)

Known as Mubarak the Great, Mubarak was the seventh ruler from the Sabah family and ruled from 1896 to 1915. He assassinated his half brother Muhammad bin Sabah to become ruler of Kuwait. Mubarak signed a treaty with the British in 1899, making Kuwait a British protectorate. He gave Britain control over Kuwait's foreign affairs and defense. The Sabah family kept control of the nation's domestic affairs, however. In return, the British provided protection against the Ottoman Empire, which had previously supported his half brother. After Mubarak's death, his successor installed a peaceable system of succession.

DOHA VILLAGE AND KUWAIT ENTERTAINMENT CITY On an arm of land jutting into Kuwait Bay, Doha Village is the location of Kuwait Entertainment City, an amusement park modeled on Disneyland. Doha Village is also home to several small dhow-building yards and a fishing village of shacks. Visitors can see crabs tunneling in the nearby mud flats.

FAYLAKAH ISLAND This island is the home of Kuwait's main archaeological site. Soldiers were the only permanent residents on this beautiful island after the first Gulf war, but the Kuwaiti government is developing tourist sites there. It is worth making the effort to view the ruins from settlements of the early Dilmun and Greek cvilizations. The main attraction of the island is its Greek temple to Artemis. Ferry boats travel to the island from Kuwait City.

THE LIBERATION TOWER (Kuwait City) The symbol of Kuwaiti freedom from the 1990–1991 Iraq invasion, the Liberation Tower is one of the tallest telecommunications towers in the world. It rises 1,220 feet (372 m) high. The tower complex includes a public communications center, revolving observation level, and a restaurant. Its elevators are among the fastest in the world at 21 feet (6.3 m) per second.

NATIONAL MUSEUM (Kuwait City) The National Museum houses one of the best collections of Islamic art in the world. Four buildings and a planetarium make up the museum complex. Iraqi invaders looted and burned the museum, but Iraq later returned most items. Holdings include pearl-diving relics and archaeological finds from Faylakah Island.

RED FORT (al-Jahrah) Also known as the Red Palace, the Red Fort is a low, rectangular structure. Its name comes from the color of its mud-brick walls. Built around a large open courtyard, the fort played a key role in the unsuccessful 1920 Saudi Arabian siege of al-Jahrah.

AL-SADU HOUSE (Kuwait City) The Bedouin lived a life governed by the rhythm of the seasons. A traditional craft of major importance was sadu weaving. Traditionally, women wove geometric designs by hand with dyed wool. In 1980 efforts to protect Bedouin crafts from dying out led to the establishment of the al-Sadu House. Exhibits depict Kuwait's old houses, mosques, and pottery. One section houses an old-fashioned roofed playground for children. Visitors can relax at Abu Adnan Café, decorated with colorful weavings.

SCIENCE AND NATURAL HISTORY MUSEUM (Kuwait City) The museum offers informative displays about Kuwait's petroleum industry as well as natural history, aviation, electronics, and zoology. A planetarium is also on site.

Arabic: the official language of Kuwait. Classical Arabic is the language of the Quran.

Bedouin: an early inhabitant of the Arabian Peninsula. The camel-herding nomads called themselves *bedu*, which the French turned into the name "Bedouin."

desalination: the process of removing salt from seawater to produce drinkable water

desert: an area that receives less than 10 inches (25 cm) of rain a year

desertification: the process of land turning into desert, caused by a combination of human and climate factors, including drought and overuse of dry lands

emir: an Arabic title that means "commander." Rulers of Kuwait and other Persian Gulf states use the title.

fundamentalist: a member of a movement within a larger group that wants strict observance of the group's basic (fundamental) principles and ideas

gross domestic product (GDP): the value of goods and services produced in a country in a year. Gross national product (GNP) also counts foreign income.

hadith: a collection of the sayings and actions of the prophet Muhammad

Islam: a worldwide religion founded through the prophet Muhammad. The holy book of Islam, the Quran, contains Muhammad's messages from Allah.

literacy: the ability to read and write a basic sentence. A country's literacy is one of the indicators of its level of development.

mosque: an Islamic place of public worship and prayer

Muslim: a follower of Islam

nomad: a herder who moves from place to place in search of pasture and water for livestock

oasis: a fertile place in the desert where underground water comes near the surface

Quran: the holy book of Islam. In Arabic, *al-Quran* means "the recitation." The prophet Muhammad dictated the book starting in A.D. 610. Muslims believe these scriptures are the word of God.

Sharia: Islamic teaching and law based on the Quran and the hadith. In Kuwait, Sharia regulates matters such as marriage, divorce, inheritance, and some criminal offenses.

sheikh: "elder" in Arabic; the clan chief in Bedouin society. Kuwait's rulers are called sheikhs.

souk: a marketplace, traditionally with specific areas for different goods and trades, such as carpets or jewelry making. Souks also sell modern goods such as DVDs.

Glossary

BBC News. 2006.
http://www.bbc.co.uk (March 2006).
The World Edition of the BBC (British Broadcasting Corporation) News is updated throughout the day, every day. The BBC is a source for comprehensive news coverage about Kuwait. It also provides a country profile at http://news .bbc.co.uk/go/pr/fr//1/hi/world/middle_east/country_profiles/791053.stm.

Canby, Thomas Y. "The Persian Gulf: After the Storm." *National Geographic*, **August 1991.**
http://www.nationalgeographic.com/ngm/100best/storyD_story.html (January 2006).
This illustrated article covers the oil fires in Kuwait after the first Persian Gulf war. Each day, flames consumed about 5 million barrels of oil. They generated more than half a million tons (500 metric tons) of pollutants. The toxins included sulfur dioxide, the key component of acid rain. Billowing 2 miles (3 km) high, the dark clouds traveled on winds far beyond Kuwait. Black rains fell in Saudi Arabia and Iran, and black snow fell in Kashmir more than 1,500 miles (2,414 km) eastward.

Central Intelligence Agency (CIA). "Kuwait." *The World Factbook.* **2006.**
http://www.cia.gov/cia/publications/factbook/geos/ku.html (January 2006).
This CIA website provides facts and figures on Kuwait's geography, people, government, economy, communications, transportation, military, and more.

Energy Information Administration. *Kuwait Country Analysis.* **June 2005.**
http://www.eia.doe.gov/emeu/cabs/kuwait.html (March 2006).
This site is one of the most complete sources of energy statistics on the Internet. It offers information about energy production and use in Kuwait and other countries of the world. The site also includes a kids' section about energy.

Gordon, Frances Linzee, Anthony Ham, Virginia Maxwell, and Jenny Walker. *Arabian Peninsula.* **Hawthorn, AUS: Lonely Planet Publications, 2004.**
Besides political and geographic information, this book offers special chapters on religion and language shared by the nations of the Arabian Peninsula, including Kuwait. The section on Kuwait outlines sights to see, transportation, and a section focusing on Kuwait City.

Gordon, Matthew. *Islam.* **Rev. ed. New York: Facts on File, 2001.**
This book, part of the World Religions series, provides an overview of Islam. It discusses the religion's history, basic beliefs, and the modern Islamic world. Illustrations and sidebars accompany the informative text.

Library of Congress, Federal Research Division. *A Country Study: Kuwait.* **1994.**
http://lcweb2.loc.gov/frd/cs/kwtoc.html (March 2006).
This country study, prepared by the U.S. Federal Research Division, covers the main historical, social, economic, political, and national security aspects of Kuwait. Sources of information include scholarly publications, official reports and documents of government and international organizations, and foreign and domestic newspapers and periodicals.

The Middle East and North Africa, 2006. **London: Routledge, 2006.**
The long section on Kuwait in this annual publication covers the country's recent history, geography, and culture. It also provides a detailed look at the economy, politics, and government of the nation. Statistics and sources are included as well. This is a volume in the Europa Regional Surveys of the World series.

O'Connell, Edward P. "A Captain's Perspective on the Gulf War," 137–165 in Michael P. Vriesenga, USAF, ed. *From the Line in the Sand: Accounts of USAF Company Grade Officers in Support of Desert Shield/Desert Storm.* Maxwell AFB, AL: Air University Press, 1994.
O'Connell's article is one of a collection of memoirs by U.S Air Force members who participated in the 1991 Gulf War.

Peck, Malcolm A. *Historical Dictionary of the Gulf Arab States.* Lanham, MD: Scarecrow Press, 1997.
A very useful reference book, this dictionary offers short articles on culture, economics, history, politics, and social issues, as well as informative entries on people, places, and events. Maps and a bibliography are included.

Population Reference Bureau. 2005.
http://www.prb.org (January 2006).
PRB provides annual, in-depth demographics on Kuwait's population. It includes birth and death rates, infant mortality rates, and other statistics relating to health, environment, education, employment, family planning, and more. Special articles cover environmental and health issues.

Robinson, Gordon, and Paul Greenway. *Bahrain, Kuwait & Qatar.* Hawthorn, AUS: Lonely Planet Publications, 2000.
Political, historical, and cultural information, maps, color photos, information about the Arabic language, and helpful travel advice are all included in this in-depth guidebook to three small Persian Gulf countries. Lonely Planet's website about Kuwait can be found at http://www.lonelyplanet.com/worldguide/destinations/middle-east/kuwait/.

Tareq Rajab Museum. 2002.
http://www.trmkt.com (March 2006).
The online site of the Tareq Rajab Museum in Kuwait City displays Islamic ceramics, costumes, jewelry, manuscripts, and metalwork. The museum is the private collection of the Rajab family. They opened their collection to the public in 1980.

U.S. Department of State, Bureau of Near Eastern Affairs. *Background Note: Kuwait.* November 2005.
http://www.state.gov/r/pa/ei/bgn/35876.htm (March 2006).
The background notes of the U.S. State Department supplies a profile of Kuwait's people, history, government, political conditions, and economy. The State Department also provides travel information for Americans going abroad.

America-Mideast Educational and Training Services, Inc. (AMIDEAST). *Kuwait.*
http://www.amideast.org/offices/kuwait/country_info.htm
AMIDEAST, based in Washington, D.C., is a nongovernmental organization that works to strengthen mutual understanding between Americans and the peoples of the Middle East. This site offers information focusing on Kuwait.

Arab Times
http://www.arabtimesonline.com
One of Kuwait's eight daily newspapers, the *Arab Times* covers politics and financial news in English.

Art of Sami Mohammed
http://www.geocities.com/SoHo/Village/3656/sami2.html
This site provides a biography of Kuwaiti artist Sami Mohammed and an online gallery of some of his sculptures and paintings.

Behnke, Alison, and Vartkes Ehramjian. *Cooking the Middle Eastern Way.* **Minneapolis: Lerner Publications Company, 2005.**
Kuwait shares many dishes with other Middle Eastern countries. Yet each nation also has its own specialties, leading to a diversity of dishes.

Dickson, H. R. P. *The Arab of the Desert.* **3rd ed., rev. and abridged edition. London: Allen & Unwin, 1983.**
Dickson (1881–1959) was a British government officer in the Gulf during World War I (1914–1918) and after. This book about Bedouin life in Kuwait and Arabia is considered a minor classic. He also wrote *Kuwait and Her Neighbors.*

Dickson, Violet. *Forty Years in Kuwait.* **London: Allen & Unwin, 1971.**
Forty Years in Kuwait is Dixon's memoir of living in Kuwait. She arrived in the country as a young bride in 1929. Her autobiography records the vast changes she saw come to the country, especially after the discovery of oil. Dickson also wrote *The Wild Flowers of Kuwait and Bahrain* (1955).

Facey, William, and Gilliam Grant. *Kuwait by the First Photographers.* **London: I. B. Tauris, 1998.**
This book documents the way of life in Kuwait between 1900 and 1950. It is a visual record of the time before fishing, boatbuilding, and trade by land and sea was replaced by the oil industry. The photos are from the collections of many famous European travelers, including Alan Villiers.

Hell on Earth: The Kuwaiti Oil Fires. **VHS. Directed by James Deckard. New York: A&E Home Video, 1991.**
This A&E Network television documentary presents the damage the Iraqi army caused when they set ablaze the Kuwaiti oil fields at the end of the 1991 Gulf War. The film also follows a firefighting team as they try to cap the raging fires.

Jelloun, Tahar Ben. *Islam Explained.* **New York: The New Press, 2004.**
This book offers a clear introduction to the history and main beliefs of Islam. Presented in a question-and-answer format, the Muslim author responds to his young daughter's questions about being Muslim in modern times. The book also defines words often heard in the news, such as terrorist, crusade, jihad, and fundamentalist.

Further Reading and Websites

Kuwait Information Office
http://www.kuwait-info.org/
This site is a resource for information about Kuwait, its rich culture and heritage, history, current events, and much more. The Kuwait Information Office in Washington, D.C., works for greater understanding of Kuwait.

O'Shea, Maria. *Kuwait*. New York: Marshall Cavendish, 1999.
This book is part of the Cultures of the World series for younger readers. It introduces the geography, history, religions, government, and people of Kuwait. Photographs and charts accompany the text.

Price Hossell, Karen. *The Persian Gulf War*. Chicago: Heinemann Library, 2003.
This is a volume in the 20th Century Perspectives series for younger readers. It explores the causes and results of the Iraqi invasion of Kuwait in 1990 and the story of the U.S.-led coalition that liberated Kuwait in 1991.

al-Shamlan, Saif Marzooq. *Pearling in the Arabian Gulf: A Kuwaiti Memoir*. Translated by Peter Clark. London: London Center for Arabic Studies, 2000.
This fascinating autobiography tells of a way of life in the early 1900s before Japanese cultured pearls replaced naturally harvested pearls. Photos add to the text.

vgsbooks.com
http://www.vgsbooks.com
Visit vgsbooks.com, the home page of the Visual Geography Series®, which is updated regularly. You can get linked to all sorts of useful online information, including geographical, historical, demographic, cultural, and economic websites. The vgsbooks.com site is a great resource for late-breaking news and statistics.

Villiers, Alan. *Sons of Sinbad; An Account of Sailing with the Arabs in Their Dhows, in the Red Sea, around the Coasts of Arabia, and to Zanzibar and Tanganyika*. New York: Scribner, 1969.
Alan Villiers (1903–1982) was a sailor, author, and photographer. Beginning in 1938, he spent one and a half years on board the Arab dhow *The Triumph of Righteousness*. He sailed near Kuwait during his trip and recorded his experience in *Sons of Sinbad*.

Zeinert, Karen and Mary Miller. *The Brave Women of the Gulf Wars*. Minneapolis: Twenty-First Century Books, 2006.
This book is part of the Women at War series. Before the first Persian Gulf war, men and women had never served together in integrated units in a war zone. The biographies of these brave women illustrate that shattering stereotypes can be achieved through simple acts of patriotism.

Zwier, Larry, and Matthew Weltig. *The Persian Gulf and Iraqi Wars*. Minneapolis: Twenty-First Century Books, 2005.
This book is part of the Chronicle of America's Wars series. In 2003 the United States entered into the second chapter of a war with Iraq begun in 1991. In the first chapter, U.S. soldiers had helped to free Kuwait from Iraqi invasion. In 2003 U.S. soldiers were again sent to the region, this time to topple the regime of Saddam Hussein.

Captions for photos appearing on cover and chapter openers:

Cover: Of the three towers known as the Kuwait City Water Towers, the tallest tower is 607 ft. (185 m) high. It houses several restaurants. The lower half of its larger sphere and the sphere on the second tower are water reservoirs. The third tower lights the others after dark.

pp. 4–5 Kuwait City's financial district includes the Kuwait Stock Exchange *(left)* and banks.

pp. 8–9 Burgan Oil Field pipelines cross Kuwait's desert.

pp. 18–19 This photograph of the archaeological excavations on Faylakah Island was taken before Iraq's 1992 invasion of Kuwait. The excavations revealed a Greek colony from the 300s B.C.

pp. 34–35 Children anticipate a thrilling ride at a neighborhood fair in Kuwait City.

pp. 46–47 Colorful carpets are rolled out for Muslim worshipers gathering to pray on the first day of Eid al-Adha in Kuwait City. Also called the Feast of Sacrifice, Eid al-Adha is a four-day Muslim holiday that follows the annual Muslim pilgrimage to Mecca, Saudi Arabia.

pp. 58–59 A California construction firm built the Kuwait Entertainment City in Doha Village near Kuwait City in the 1970s. The cost of the complex was $35 million.

Photo Acknowledgments

The images in this book are used with the permission of: © Helene Rogers/Art Directors, pp. 4–5, 8–9, 39, 43, 44, 56, 60; © XNR Productions, pp. 6, 10; Department of Defense, p. 13; © Ken Lucas/Visuals Unlimited, p. 15; © Trip/Art Directors, pp. 18–19; © North Wind Picture Archives, p. 21; © Three Lions/Getty Images, p. 25; © Romeo Gacad/AFP/Getty Images, p. 26; Defense Visual Information Center, p. 28; © Bob Pearson/AFP/Getty Images, p. 30; © Yasser Al-Zayyat/AFP/Getty Images, p. 32; © Joe Raedle/Getty Images, pp. 34–35, 46–47, 49; © www.copix.co.uk/R.Bell, p. 37; © Charles Walker/Topfoto/The Image Works, pp. 41, 55; © Stewart Innes/ZUMA Press, p. 42; © G. Frysinger/Travel-Images.com, p. 51; © Juliet Highet/Art Directors, pp. 52, 58–59; © www.copix.co.uk/Christine Osborne, pp. 53, 62; Audrius Tomonis—www.banknotes.com, p. 68; © Laura Westlund/Independent Picture Service, p. 69.

Front Cover: © Helene Rogers/Art Directors. Back Cover: NASA.